The Story of Cinderella

A Pantomime

Ronald Parr

A Samuel French Acting Edition

SAMUELFRENCH-LONDON.CO.UK
SAMUELFRENCH.COM

Copyright © 1954 by Ronald Parr
All Rights Reserved

THE STORY OF CINDERELLA is fully protected under the copyright laws of the British Commonwealth, including Canada, the United States of America, and all other countries of the Copyright Union. All rights, including professional and amateur stage productions, recitation, lecturing, public reading, motion picture, radio broadcasting, television and the rights of translation into foreign languages are strictly reserved.

ISBN 978-0-573-06418-0

www.samuelfrench-london.co.uk

www.samuelfrench.com

For Amateur Production Enquiries

United Kingdom and World excluding North America

plays@SamuelFrench-London.co.uk

020 7255 4302/01

Each title is subject to availability from Samuel French, depending upon country of performance.

CAUTION: Professional and amateur producers are hereby warned that *THE STORY OF CINDERELLA* is subject to a licensing fee. Publication of this play does not imply availability for performance. Both amateurs and professionals considering a production are strongly advised to apply to the appropriate agent before starting rehearsals, advertising, or booking a theatre. A licensing fee must be paid whether the title is presented for charity or gain and whether or not admission is charged.

The professional rights in this play are controlled by Samuel French Ltd, 52 Fitzroy Street, London, W1T 5JR.

No one shall make any changes in this title for the purpose of production. No part of this book may be reproduced, stored in a retrieval system, or transmitted in any form, by any means, now known or yet to be invented, including mechanical, electronic, photocopying, recording, videotaping, or otherwise, without the prior written permission of the publisher. No one shall upload this title, or part of this title, to any social media websites.

The right of Ronald Parr to be identified as author of this work has been asserted by him in accordance with Section 77 of the Copyright, Designs and Patents Act 1988

CHARACTERS

PRINCE CHARMING
DANDINI, equerry to Prince Charming
BARON HARDUP
BUTTONS, domestic staff of Hardup Hall
AN ATTENDANT
RUDOLF, ex-King of Pandemonium
HON. HILDA HARDUP, his eldest daughter
TILDA HARDUP, his second daughter
CINDERELLA, his youngest daughter
MISS MABEL MABB, M.A.
FAIRY FAY, her assistant
1ST FAIRY
ELVES, FAIRIES, COURT GUESTS

SYNOPSIS OF SCENES

ACT I

Scene 1	*The Magic Shop*
Scene 2	*A Woodland Glade*
Scene 3	*The Kitchen of Hardup Hall*
Scene 4	*The Woodland Glade*
Scene 5	*The Kitchen of Hardup Hall*

ACT II

Scene 1	*The Road to the Palace*
Scene 2	*The Ballroom of the Palace*
Scene 3	*The Woodland Glade*
Scene 4	*The Kitchen of Hardup Hall*
Scene 5	*The Way to the Magic Shop*
Scene 6	*The Magic Shop*
Scene 7	*The Ballroom of the Palace*

AUTHOR'S NOTE

The Story of Cinderella was first produced by John Harrison at Nottingham Playhouse on 23rd December 1952. Its second production was by Harry Lomax at The Coliseum, Oldham, on 26th December 1953.

The version lends itself equally to a simple or elaborate production. Stage directions, given from the actors' viewpoint, may freely be modified according to local conditions and inspirations. The main point to be remembered is that the essential humour of this type of burlesque lies in incongruities of which the characters are unaware. The more earnestly the players pursue their odd occasions, the funnier they will seem.

R. P.

SYNOPSIS OF MUSICAL NUMBERS

(From the Operas of Sir Arthur Sullivan)

ACT I

SCENE 2

1. Song of the Ex-Demon King — RUDOLF
Tune: *When the Night Wind Howls*
(*Ruddigore*)

SCENE 3

2a. Ballad — BUTTONS
Tune: *Tit-willow* (*The Mikado*)

2b. Duet verse, No. 2a — BUTTONS *and* CINDERELLA

SCENE 5

3. Song — CINDERELLA
Tune: *I'm called Little Buttercup*
(*H.M.S. Pinafore*)

ACT II

SCENE 1

4. Patter Trio — HARDUP, HILDA *and* TILDA
Tune: *My Eyes are Fully Opened*
(*Ruddigore*)

SCENE 2

5. Gavotte (*The Gondoliers*) — BALL GUESTS
6. Trio — DANDINI, PRINCE, RUDOLF
Tune: *as No. 3*
7. Song — DANDINI
Tune: *The Flowers that Bloom* (*The Mikado*)
8. Ballad — CINDERELLA
Tune: *Ah, Leave Me Not to Pine*
(*Pirates of Penzance*)

SCENE 3

9. Chorus Song — MISS MABB *and* FAIRY FAY
Tune: *When a Felon's Not Engaged*
(*Pirates of Penzance*)

SYNOPSIS OF MUSICAL NUMBERS

SCENE 4
   10 Duet   CINDERELLA *and*
         Tune: *Prithee, Pretty Maiden* (*Patience*)   RUDOLF

SCENE 7
   11 Duet   DANDINI *and*
         Tune: *A Waterloo House Young Man*   RUDOLF
         (*Patience*)
   12 Finale *Tune as No. 3*   FULL COMPANY

All the music needed for use in this Pantomime is now out of copyright in its original form, the composer having been dead for more than fifty years. The composer's original work may therefore be used without permission or payment. But, in the case of some items, there may be new arrangements that are subject to copyright, and if any of these copyright arrangements are used permission must be sought in the usual way from the publishers of the music or from the Performing Rights Society. Permission to perform the Pantomime does not include permission to use copyright arrangements of the music.

CINDERELLA

ACT I

SCENE I

SCENE.—*The Magic Shop.*
The shop is a blend of village store and the apothecary's shop in "Romeo and Juliet". There is an open window LC *of the back wall, with a door* R *of it. There are lots of boxes, tins, jars and sacks, also a rack containing several empty coat-hangers. Some of these are stacked* R, *others are on a counter which runs down the* L *wall. A pile of witches' broomsticks is set under the window. There is another door down* L. *Large cobwebs suggest that trade is not brisk.*

When the CURTAIN *rises,* FAIRY FAY, *a pert young fairy, is asleep on the counter. The door up stage is opened and closed by an invisible hand.* FAIRY FAY *starts up and slides from the counter.*

FAIRY FAY (*still half-asleep*) Good morning, madam. And what can I have the pleasure of . . . (*Looking round*) Surely I heard someone come in?

(MISS MABB *appears in a puff of smoke. She is an eccentric but dignified elderly fairy*)

MISS MABB. You did. (*She hangs up her cloak and wings*)
FAIRY FAY. Oh, so it's you, Miss Mabb. And I thought you were a customer at last.
MISS MABB. As I might well have been. I've told you before, Miss Fay, I will not have the sales staff asleep on the counter. It gives a distinct impression of slackness.
FAIRY FAY. No wonder! We haven't sold a thing since the spring sales and now it's nearly Christmas.
MISS MABB. I know there isn't the money about these days. But that's no excuse for neglecting your work.
FAIRY FAY. Work? There just isn't any to neglect!
MISS MABB. Nonsense! How long is it since you took stock?
FAIRY FAY. Only a week. And nothing's been touched since then.
MISS MABB (*blowing dust off the counter*) So I see! Well, we'll just check up if you don't mind. Come along, out with your stock-book. Now, write these down while I count. . . . Ten single witch-power flying broomsticks.
FAIRY FAY (*writing in the stock-book*) Ten single w.p. flying broomsticks.

(*A broomstick flies out of the window or door*)

MISS MABB (*calmly*) Correction. Nine single witch-power flying broomsticks. (*Shutting the window/door*) How often must I tell you to keep this window/door closed? Now, what's next? Ah—one dozen gallon jars of baboon's blood for cooling cauldrons.

FAIRY FAY. One doz. bab. blood for c.c.

MISS MABB. Forty-nine fillets of fenney snake for potent potions—(*sniffing*) h'm, they don't smell as fresh as they did. How long have we had them in stock?

FAIRY FAY (*consulting the book*) Three hundred and fifty-seven years.

MISS MABB. H'm. They *should* be all right. Still, better mark them down from five shillings to four-and-eleven. Got that?

FAIRY FAY. O.K.

(MISS MABB *brings a bale of cloth from under the counter*)

MISS MABB. Seventeen yards of best-quality hand-woven spells, thirty-six inches wide, assorted traditional patterns . . .

FAIRY FAY. Seventeen yards . . .

MISS MABB (*counting the coat-hangers*) Six invisible cloaks . . . Just a moment, I think I hear someone coming. (*She peeps through the window*) Yes, it *is* someone.

FAIRY FAY. Who? A customer?

MISS MABB. Looks more like a commercial traveller. Bother! I can't waste time on *him* this morning.

FAIRY FAY (*going behind the counter*) Leave him to me—I'll soon get rid of him.

MISS MABB. Do! I'll just go and pop a potion in the pressure cooker.

(MISS MABBS *exits* L)

FAIRY FAY. Trust me to hold the fort.

(RUDOLF *swaggers in up* RC. *Formerly the Demon King of Pandemomium, his attire now suggests the Wicked Squire of Victorian melodrama. But his eyes still flash with infernal fire, and his top hat is ingeniously designed to accommodate a neat pair of horns*)

RUDOLF (*with grating politeness*) Good morning! May I see the proprietress?

FAIRY FAY (*aloofly*) Sorry, I'm afraid you can't.

RUDOLF. Oh? Why not? Is she out?

FAIRY FAY. No, she's in-visible. She's always invisible to commercials on Wednesdays.

RUDOLF. Commercials? Young woman, I ask you! Do I *look* like a commercial?

FAIRY FAY (*considering*) W-e-l-l—yes, you do rather.

RUDOLF (*stiffly, offering a visiting card*) Me card!

SCENE I   THE STORY OF CINDERELLA   3

FAIRY FAY (*taking it*) What's this? His Majesty King Rudolf of Pandemonium! Then—you are the Demon King himself.
RUDOLF. I am. (*Becoming uneasy*) That is, I was. There was a spot of bother and I had to abdicate.
FAIRY FAY. Oh yes. I remember reading about it in the *News of the Underworld*.
RUDOLF. You mustn't believe all you read in the Sunday papers. All I did was to raise a whir-r-r-lwind without consulting the Ministry of Storms and Tempest. But now you know who I am, perhaps you'll let me see your employer—this Mabb person.

(MISS MABB *enters* L)

MISS MABB. Miss Mabel Mabb, M.A., if you please!
RUDOLF. Oh, and what does M.A. stand for? Magical Arts?
MISS MABB. Certainly not! I am a Mistress of Abracadabra of the University of Fairyland.
RUDOLF. Really? Of course I'm a 'varsity man meself. In fact, I'm an Old Blue Devil.
MISS MABB. Indeed? And what, may I ask, is your ex-Majesty doing nowadays?
RUDOLF. You'll find the answer on me card.
FAIRY FAY (*showing the card to Miss Mabb*) Look! It says "Managing Director, Magical Monopolies Unlimited."
MISS MABB. What? Those destroyers of sound tradition and honest craftsmanship?
RUDOLF. Ah, but just wait till you see our next balance sheet! We shall pay a thousand per cent.
MISS MABB. But to do that you would have to own all the magic in this Land of Fairytale.
RUDOLF. Precisely. And that explains the object of me visit. (*He produces a document*) All you have to do is to sign on the dotted line.
MISS MABB (*reading the document*) This is too much! He wants to buy me up and close me down!

(RUDOLF *counts out notes with a flourish*)

FAIRY FAY (*reading the document*) "Received for stock and goodwill of the Magic Shop, twenty pounds in cash . . ." What, only twenty pounds?
RUDOLF. More than it's worth, if you ask me. Still, I can afford to be generous. Well, is it a deal?
MISS MABB. Does your ex-Majesty realize how long I've been building up this business?
RUDOLF. Quite a while, I fancy.
MISS MABB. On Tuesday week it will be exactly three thousand two hundred and seventeen years.
RUDOLF. Really? Well then, isn't it about time you began to take things more easily?

MISS MABB. Sir, rather than surrender my life's work to you I would toil on until beset by old age and infirmity.
RUDOLF. Madam, be reasonable! How can you hope to compete with an up-to-date organization like mine? Look at these flying brooms, for instance. All last century's model.
MISS MABB. But surely what was good enough for my late aunt, the illustrious Queen Mab herself . . .
RUDOLF. Isn't good enough for the ordinary working fairy of today. All *our* broomsticks are jet-propelled. *These* won't even break through the light barrier. Tell me, do you sell 'em on the never-never?
MISS MABB. Never, ever! My price is ten pounds cash down.
RUDOLF. There you are! Who'd pay ten pounds when you can fly away on one of our broomsticks after a first payment of ten bob?
MISS MABB. And then?
RUDOLF. Oh, ten bob a week for the next two hundred years—and the broomstick's yours.
MISS MABB (*seizing and brandishing a broom*) Sheer moonlight robbery! So you despise my broomsticks, do you? Out of my shop, you villain, before I give you a free sample!

(FAIRY FAY *mounts the counter in alarm*)

RUDOLF. I warn you, I can still raise a whirlwind or two!
MISS MABB. And my broomsticks can ride 'em!

(DANDINI, *a dapper and sprightly courtier, enters just in time to prevent a fight*)

DANDINI. I say, am I interrupting something?
MISS MABB. Oh, no, I was only giving him the brush-off!
DANDINI. So sorry, but it's top priority. I'm Dandini, you know—the Prince's equerry and P.R.O. And I've a message to deliver in person to Baron Hardup of Hardup Hall.
MISS MABB. The eminent inventor? Why, he's my landlord!
DANDINI. Really? I hear the Baron has a couple of attractive girls.
MISS MABB. Oh dear, no! Baron Hardup has only *one* attractive daughter.
DANDINI. Then someone's made a nonsense of these ball invitations.
MISS MABB. What's this? Another ball at the Palace?
DANDINI. Yes—tonight. The Prince has been quite depressed lately and we want to cheer him up. So I'm taking invitations to all the well-connected girls in the Land of Fairytale. These are for the Honourable Hilda Hardup and Miss Tilda Hardup. (*He shows the invitations*)
RUDOLF (*heavily aside*) Ah! I wonder what they keep under the counter? (*He hides under it*)

Scene I   THE STORY OF CINDERELLA   5

Miss Mabb. But Hilda and Tilda are the *un*-attractive daughters.
Dandini. Then who's the attractive one?
Miss Mabb. Their stepsister and my godchild, dear little Cinderella.
Dandini. Cinderella? What a peculiar name! Anyway, I'm afraid it isn't on my list.
Miss Mabb. Then put it on, man, put it on!
Dandini (*writing*) Oh, very well. The more the merrier, I suppose. Cin-der-ella! And now, perhaps you can tell me how I get to Hardup Hall?
Miss Mabb. Straight on to the cross-roads—then close your eyes, turn round three times, wait for the green light, and follow your instincts.
Dandini. Oh, I always do that. Good-bye.

(Dandini *bows and goes out*)

Miss Mabb. Good-bye, young man—and mind you invite Cinderella to the ball. (*Turning round*) Well, that's settled *him*—and now to settle with . . . Hello! Where's his ex-Majesty?
Fairy Fay (*looking under the counter, etc.*) He seems to have gone.
Miss Mabb. Lucky for him!

(Rudolf's *chuckle is heard*)

Fairy Fay. What was that?
Miss Mabb. I heard nothing.
Fairy Fay. Sounded like a chuckle.
Miss Mabb. Young woman, you're far too imaginative for a working fairy.
Fairy Fay. Miss Mabb—do you suppose Rudolf *could* turn us out of the Magic Shop?
Miss Mabb. Of course he couldn't! Only Baron Hardup could do that—and he'd never dream of such a thing.
Fairy Fay. Perhaps not—but you know what a lot of money he needs for his inventions. And after all, we are a little behind with the rent.
Miss Mabb. Only forty-nine years.
Fairy Fay. But suppose the Baron had to sell his estate to raise some more money. Then we should have a new landlord, shouldn't we?
Miss Mabb. Yes, I suppose we should.
Fairy Fay. And if he sold it to Rudolf, then Rudolf would be our new landlord, wouldn't he?
Miss Mabb. Yes, I suppose he would.
Fairy Fay. And then he could turn us out, couldn't he?
Miss Mabb. Yes, I suppose he . . . Child, what are you saying? Not another word! Why, if Rudolf could hear you . . .

(Rudolf's *scornful laughter is heard*)

FAIRY FAY. What was that?
MISS MABB. It couldn't be, of course. But it *sounded* like . . .
BOTH. Rudolf!
MISS MABB. Come out, you skulking scoundrel!

(*The laughter grows and* RUDOLF *reappears*)

RUDOLF. Nothing under the counter! No wonder business is bad!
MISS MABB. No doubt your ex-Majesty thinks yourself very clever.
RUDOLF. Not nearly as clever as this young lady. (*To Fairy Fay*) Congratulations, my dear! I couldn't have thought of a better plan meself!

(FAIRY FAY *runs to* MISS MABB, *who embraces her protectively*)

FAIRY FAY. Oh, Miss Mabb, please forgive me!
RUDOLF. As it happens I already hold a mortgage on Baron Hardup's estate. Sooner or later he won't be able to pay the interest. Then I shall take over and kick the lot of you out. All, that is, except Cinderella!
MISS MABB. My beloved godchild! If you dare to harm a hair of her head . . .
RUDOLF. Oh, I shan't do that. I'm far too fond of dear little Cinderella. So fond of her, in fact, that I intend to marry her.
MISS MABB. What? Cinderella marry a demon of your age and reputation? Do you suppose she would ever consent?
RUDOLF. Cinderella would consent to anything to save her father from ruin.
MISS MABB. Not while I am here to protect her.
RUDOLF. Don't be ridiculous! What power has a silly old fairy like you against an influential demon like me?
MISS MABB. Old I may be. But in these veins there boils the blood of my imperial relative, Queen Mab. Ex-King Rudolf, I defy you!
RUDOLF. It is war between us, then?
MISS MABB. War to the end!
RUDOLF. So be it!

(*Storm music with effects. During* RUDOLF'S *invocation,* MISS MABB *signs to* FAIRY FAY *who hastily arrays her in her M.A. robes, bearing magic signs, and hands her her Wand. It is rather a scramble but the final result is impressive*)

(*through the music*) Spirits of the vasty deep,
     Hear your lord and leave your sleep!
     Hither on the whirlwind fly
     Darkening the winter sky:
     Black eclipse and lightning flash,

SCENE I   THE STORY OF CINDERELLA   7

> Flood and flame and thunder-crash;
> Tropic rain and Arctic hail,
> Steeple-shaking gust and gale
> On this fragile roof descend,
> These presumptuous lives to end!

(*The storm has reached its height. But now* MISS MABB *is fully arrayed and ready to reply. During her invocation the storm abates and* FAIRIES *and* ELVES *rush in, mount themselves on broomsticks, and chase* RUDOLF *round the room*)

MISS MABB. Fairies of the field and glade,
Rally quickly to the aid
Of Miss Mabel Mabb, M.A.:
Drive the Demon King away;
Each upon her magic broom
Sweep this rubbish from the room:
Fairies of the upper air,
Change the weather-glass to "Fair";
Calm the tempest, clear the sky;
You can do it if you try!
Now, all together—that's the stuff!

RUDOLF. All right, I'm off—I've had enough!

(RUDOLF *backs out of the door but immediately reappears at the window*)

> Next time we meet, my clever friend,
> The tale will have a different end!
> Beware! Beware! Beware! Beware!

(RUDOLF *disappears from the window*)

MISS MABB. Thanks, fairies of the earth and air:
That makes your good deed for today—
Now you may run along and play.
FAIRY FAY. But what about poor Cinderella?
I think that someone ought to tell her
That wicked Rudolf's on her trail.
MISS MABB. She shall have warning without fail!

(*To the Audience*)

> Children, will you all help, my dears?
> Whenever Rudolf tells a lie
> He always winks a wicked eye;
> So watch him carefully, and when
> You catch the rascal winking, then
> It's time to give a warning hiss—
> That is to say a noise like this:

(*All demonstrate hissing*)
Easily done, as you can see—
Come, try it over now with me!
(*More hissing*)
That's very good! Now, one more try—
I'll tell you what, pretend that I
Am Rudolf. Now, let's see if you
Can all remember what to do.
(*She strikes an attitude in imitation of Rudolf, and is hissed by all*)
That's really splendid. In this way
Each one of you can help our play,
And earn dear Cinders' thanks and kisses
By giving Rudolf hearty hisses.

(RUDOLF *appears at the window. Everyone hisses*)

CURTAIN

SCENE 2

SCENE—*A Woodland Glade.*
This scene is played in front of TABS.
When the CURTAIN *rises,* RUDOLF *enters* L.

No. 1   SONG OF THE EX-DEMON KING (RUDOLF)

RUDOLF.
I used to be his Majesty the King of the Demon Land,
A potentate with powers great in my demoniac hand;
To cut a dash with a lightning flash or a thunderbolt or two
Was the kind of thing that the Demon King was privileged to do.
   Hoorah for the Demon King!
    The Demon King!
   Hoorah for the Demon King!
I loved to wake a wild earthquake and watch the people run
As the trembling town came crashing down on top of everyone,
Or to lash the main with a hurricane a-howling a horrid tune
Till I sank a fleet, for a special treat of a Saturday afternoon.
   A-howling a horrid tune!
    A-howling,
   A-howling a horrid tune!

(*During the last verse* MISS MABB *enters, followed by* FAIRIES)

Scene 3   THE STORY OF CINDERELLA   9

But it was my fate to abdicate, and now as you can see
A plutocrat in a big top-hat I'm quite content to be:
When you've had your fling as a Demon King it's pleasant to
   retire,
And to settle down in a country town as a Fearfully Wicked
   Squire.

    Miss Mabb. Beware of the Wicked Squire!
    Fairies (*hissing to music*) S-s-s-s-s-s!
    Rudolf (*retreating*) Take the curse of the Wicked Squire.

Curtain

Scene 3

Scene—*The Kitchen of Hardup Hall.*
It has a vaguely Tudor appearance, with fantastic beams and a big fireplace R. *There are doors up* R, *to the courtyard, and* L *to the rest of the Hall, and a window up* RC. *Baron Hardup's inventive genius and untidiness are everywhere apparent. Up* LC *is his Fairyvision set, surmounted by a large screen. This may be of gauze, transparent when lit from behind; or more simply a curtain which can be drawn when the set is "tuned in". A crazy series of kitchen units, with many doors, contrived from biscuit-tins and other oddments stands up* L. *Attached is an automatic washing-machine, from which dangle sleeves ending in a pair of enormous hands. In fact these are gloves; the machine is worked by an unseen stage-hand who puts his arms in the sleeves from behind. Otherwise the kitchen is sparely furnished with a few stools, etc.*

As the Curtain *rises the* Baron *is putting the final touches—rather heavy ones—to his Fairyvision set. He wears overalls, muffler and coronet. Scattered beside him is his tool kit, including a big saw and mallet, etc. Open on the floor is a big book of instructions. After a few moments' business* Buttons *enters* L. *Over his traditional page's uniform he wears a dainty parlour-maid's uniform. He carries a pile of dirty crockery, which he deposits beside the washing-machine before turning to watch the Baron, who has been too absorbed to notice his entrance.*

    Buttons. Hello? More inventions? And what's his lordship up to this time?
    Baron Hardup (*from his speech, clearly a Northerner*) Ah, Buttons-me-lad, you may well ask! You come and have a look at this.

    (Buttons *complies, scratching his head*)

Now, guess what it is.
    Buttons. Another washing-machine?

B

HARDUP. Nay, I've made enough o' them. I'll tell you what yon is. Yon's a Fairyvision.
BUTTONS. *Fairy*vision?
HARDUP. Aye, that's what I call it—Fairyvision, patent applied for.
BUTTONS. Sure you don't mean *Tele*vision?
HARDUP. Nay, television only shows you them chaps muckin' about at Lime Grove. Well, I mean, you get tired of 'em, don't you? Now, with my Fairyvision you can take a peep at owt you fancy.
BUTTONS. Go on!
HARDUP. Aye, you can an' all—that's to say you will be able to when I've mackled it up a bit. Aye, it still wants a bit o' macklin'. (*He "mackles" vigorously*)
BUTTONS. I believe you.
HARDUP. All you do is just dial a number! (*He demonstrates*)
BUTTONS (*accusingly*) Here, you've pinched that from off the telephone!
HARDUP. Well, chap from Post Office said he'd cut it off today, so I've just saved him trouble. First you dial, like this—then you turn this handle, like this. Mind you, I don't say it's finished yet . . .

(*An alarming explosion comes from the Fairyvision set*)

BUTTONS. It's finished now.
HARDUP. Nay, it only wants a bit o' macklin'. (*He looks round*) Now, where's me book of instructions? Pass it over, there's a good lad.
BUTTONS (*picking up the book and reading the title*) *One Hundred Things a Bright Boy Can Do*. I should have thought you'd have done all those at your time of life.
HARDUP (*taking the book*) Nay, lad, I've done more than book says. Sithee here! (*He shows the book*) Now, here it shows you "How to Make a Telescope". And here's a piece on "How to Make Your Own Radio". And here's another on "How to Make a Home Cinema". Well, I tell you what I've done. I've mixed 'em all up—here a bit o' one, there a bit o' t'other—and the grand and glorious result is . . .
HARDUP }
BUTTONS } (*together*) Fairyvision!
HARDUP (*attacking the Fairyvision with the mallet*) Aye, an' a beautiful delicate sensitive piece o' mechanism it is, too—only wants a bit o' macklin'!
BUTTONS. We all know you're a genius, Baron. But why don't you invent something for paying people their wages?
HARDUP (*astonished*) Wages? Wages, did you say?

(BUTTONS *nods his head vigorously*)

Why, lad, didn't I pay you last Saturday?

(BUTTONS *changes the nod to a shake, which he continues during the rest of the Baron's questions*)

Nor the Saturday before that? Nor last quarter day? Eh, I never! Here, hold on, lad! Just you wait till I've made a fortune out o' Fairyvision and I'll double your wages.

BUTTONS. Double my pension, you mean.

HARDUP. Nay, lad, it won't be that long. As soon as I've mackled this up a bit we'll have a grand demonstration.

(TILDA HARDUP *rushes in chased by the* HON. HILDA HARDUP. *Tilda is a tall, silly, giggling girl who cannot pronounce her R's. The Hon. Hilda is short and militant, with an excessively refined accent. The* BARON, *busy with his Fairyvision, ignores the disturbance which follows*)

HILDA. Take them off, do you hear? Take them off this minute!
TILDA. Shan't! Shan't till you give me back my hair-gwips!
HILDA. The things I have to put up with in this house!
TILDA. Old meanie! She's got my hair-gwips!
HILDA. She's wearing my fifteen-deniers! Return them at once or I shall forget that I'm a lady!

(TILDA *puts out her tongue at Hilda*)

All right! I've forgotten!

(HILDA *and* TILDA *fly at each other.* BUTTONS *tries to separate them*)

BUTTONS. Here, break it up—break it up! I'm surprised at you, I am really—great big girls like you! Why can't you be more like your little sister?

TILDA. Cindewella? Why, she's just a teen-ager with an infewiowity complex!

HILDA. Doesn't even paint her toe-nails.

BUTTONS. Why, Cinders is worth the two of you put together!

TILDA. You only say that because you want to be her boy fwiend. Look, he's blushing!

HILDA. Is this true, Buttons? How dare you aspire to be my brother-in-law?

BUTTONS. I'd even put up with that if only Cinders would marry me.

HILDA. Enough! Buttons, you are dismissed. Take a month's salary in lieu of notice.

BUTTONS (*extending his hand*) Done!

HILDA. On second thoughts, you can just take a month's notice.

BUTTONS. That makes six months' notice you've given me in a fortnight.

HILDA. If I like I'll give you twelve months' notice!
TILDA. Serve you wight!
BUTTONS. What, another twelve months' hard?
HILDA. And no remission of sentence for good conduct!

(CINDERELLA *enters* R *carrying a shopping-basket*)

BUTTONS. What a life! If it wasn't for Cinders I'd—why, here she is!
HILDA. Cinderella! Where on earth have you been, child?
CINDERELLA. Shopping, of course. Somebody has to think about dinner.
HILDA. You know very well that's *my* responsibility. Why, *I've* been thinking about dinner ever since breakfast!

(*The Fairyvision set splutters and crackles.* BARON HARDUP *becomes excited*)

HARDUP. Hear that, Buttons-me-lad? It's working—Fairyvision's working!
HILDA. Don't tell us you've invented something that works.
HARDUP. Works? Of course Fairyvision works!
CINDERELLA. Fairyvision? Sounds exciting. May we have a demonstration, please?
HARDUP. Of course you can, love. Now then, everybody, just pretend you're at the pictures.

(HILDA, TILDA, CINDERELLA *and* BUTTONS *draw up stools as light glows from the FV screen*)

TILDA. How thwilling! Will we see Mawlon Bwando?
HARDUP. You can see owt you fancy.
CINDERELLA. Can we really, Father? How lovely!
HARDUP. 'Course you can, now I've mackled it up.
HILDA. How about a peep at the Palace Beautiful?
CINDERELLA. The Palace Beautiful? But—that's where Prince Charming lives—the noblest man in the Land of Fairytale.
HILDA. The richest man in the Land of Fairytale.
TILDA. Evewy girl's wish-fulfilment! Show us, Daddy!
HARDUP. Private apartments, Palace Beautiful. Let's see, that'll be Marble Hall one-two-three-four.
CINDERELLA. But—won't that be spying on his Royal Highness?
HILDA. Nonsense! A cat may look at a king.
BUTTONS. Trust you to know your rights!
HILDA. Buttons, take a month's . . .
HARDUP. Quiet, there!

(*The Fairyvision starts to buzz*)

Ladies and gentlemen, the magic carpet of Fairyvision wafts you

Scene 3   THE STORY OF CINDERELLA   13

to the private apartments of his Royal Highness Prince Charming.
TILDA. I wonder what the Pwince is doing.
BUTTONS. Having a bath, I shouldn't wonder.
HARDUP. In which case my patent blue-pencil dim-out device comes into instant operation. Hello, here we are!

(PRINCE CHARMING *appears on the Fairyvision screen*)

TILDA. The Pwince, the Pwince! (*Jumping up and waving*) Oo-oo! Pwincey!

(HILDA *slaps her*)

HARDUP (*in a "toastmaster's" voice*) I crave silence for his Royal Highness.
PRINCE. At last! A royal holiday
　　　　With no foundation stones to lay,
　　　　No loyal breasts to decorate,
　　　　No bothersome affairs of state,
　　　　No dreary documents to sign:
　　　　I stayed in bed till half past nine
　　　　And read my speeches in the papers,
　　　　Then cut a few informal capers—
　　　　It is undignified, no doubt,
　　　　But luckily no-one's about;
　　　　No courtiers to fawn or flatter
　　　　And spoil my musings with their chatter,
　　　　No literary governess
　　　　To spill the story to the Press
　　　　Of how a royal prince enjoys
　　　　His holiday like other boys.

(*He takes snuff, picks up a newspaper, throws it aside, and yawns*)

TILDA. Oo, what lovely legs!
HILDA. What delicate diction!
CINDERELLA. What a kind face!
BUTTONS. What's he got that I haven't got? Don't tell me!
HILDA. Silence! He's going to speak again.
CINDERELLA. Look, his mood has changed! Why, I don't believe he's enjoying his holiday any more!
PRINCE. Yet ah, how soon my spirits fall
　　　　As solitary pleasures pall!
　　　　Alas, will no-one tell me where
　　　　To find some lovely girl who'll share
　　　　The trials of a royal life
　　　　As my beloved queen and wife?
　　　　I pause . . . (*He pau...s*)
HILDA. Just the situation I've been looking for!

TILDA. What about me, your Woyal Highness? I've had expewience—I've been a queen alweady!
HILDA. Yes—Tractor Queen of Dagenham.*
TILDA. For thwee years wunning!
HILDA. Nineteen-eleven to nineteen-thirteen.
PRINCE. I pause—but not for a reply
   Since none can hear my anguished cry,
   O who will share my heart and throne
   And love me for myself alone?
   This melancholy put to rout ...

(*Fairyvision abruptly fades out*)

HARDUP. That's done it—battery's conked out!
HILDA. Why, he's gone!
TILDA. I've lost him! I've lost my dweam-boy! (*She weeps noisily*)
HILDA. Get him back at once, Father.
CINDERELLA. What's happened?
HARDUP. Run out o' juice, love.
CINDERELLA. What sort of juice?
HARDUP. And I thought I gave you a scientific education! Pumpkin juice, o' course—an' I'll need a couple o' mouse's whiskers. Go and fetch 'em, Buttons, there's a good lad.
BUTTONS. All right—but I'm sure I don't see what all the fuss is about.

(BUTTONS *exits* L)

HILDA. Really, Father! The first useful thing you invent and it breaks down at the critical moment!
HARDUP. Don't whittle, lass! I'll mackle it up again before you can say Prince Charming. (*He takes off his coronet and mops his brow with a handkerchief*)
CINDERELLA. Prince Charming! What a beautiful name!
HILDA. And what's he to a cinder-slut like you?

(*A knock is heard*)

There, look alive, girl! Someone at the door!
CINDERELLA (*dreamily*)
   "O who will share my heart and throne
   And love me for myself alone?"
HILDA. Do you hear, Cinders? Stop reciting poetry and answer the door at once!
CINDERELLA (*coming to with a start*) Oh dear! I expect it's that dreadful Squire Rudolf wanting his money. Luckily we've got it this time. (*She picks up a jar on the kitchen unit*)
HILDA. That's a change! (*Aside*) So *that's* where the sly puss keeps it!

* Local industry will supply an alternative title.

SCENE 3   THE STORY OF CINDERELLA

TILDA. Howwid Squire Wudolf, always after ickle Tilda's pocket-money! (*Peeping through the window*) Why, it isn't Squire Wudolf at all! It's a vewy awistocwatic young man!
HILDA. Indeed? Then *I'll* answer the door!

(HILDA *brushes aside* CINDERELLA, *who replaces the jar, and opens the door.*
DANDINI *enters.* BARON HARDUP *comes forward*)

DANDINI. Good morning! I suppose this is Hardup Hall?
HARDUP. That's right, young man.
DANDINI (*looking round*) Another of our stately mansions going to rack and ruin! Why don't you offer it to the National Trust?
HARDUP. We'd get a better price from the National Coal Board.
DANDINI. Indeed? And who are you—the gardener?
HARDUP. Look here, young feller . . .
HILDA. Father, your coronet!

(CINDERELLA *helps the* BARON *on with his coronet*)

DANDINI. Oh, I beg your pardon, Baron! On behalf of His Royal Highness Prince Charming——
CINDERELLA ⎤   ⎧ The Prince!
HILDA   ⎬ (*together*) ⎨ His Royal Highness!
TILDA   ⎦   ⎩ (*jumping*) Pwincie! Pwincie!

(*During* DANDINI's *next speech* BUTTONS *returns*)

DANDINI. —I have the honour to invite your daughters to a ball to be given this evening at the Palace Beautiful.

(*Sensation*)

Guests will be received by his Royal Highness in person. Cabaret, licensed buffet, music by Willie Witchboy and his Nine Broomsticks. Now, which is the Honourable Hilda Hardup?
HILDA. Here!
DANDINI. Your invitation, ma'am. (*He gives her an invitation*) Miss Tilda Hardup?
TILDA. One for ickle Tilda! (*She takes her invitation*)
DANDINI. The name of a third Miss Hardup has been mentioned. A most peculiar name.
CINDERELLA. I don't suppose—I mean, it couldn't possibly by any chance . . .
DANDINI. What's that, little girl? Speak up!
BUTTONS. Haven't they asked Cinderella?
DANDINI. Cinderella! That's it! But—surely *this* little girl isn't Cinderella?
CINDERELLA. Oh, but I am!
HILDA. Ridiculous! Of course there's been a mistake!
DANDINI. My dear, I wouldn't hurt your feelings for the world, but I'm afraid your sister's right. Frankly, you wouldn't do at all.

CINDERELLA. Wouldn't I?
DANDINI. Oh, no. For one thing you're far too young to stay up so late.
HARDUP. Nay, it wouldn't hurt the lass just this once.
DANDINI. Besides—forgive my mentioning it, but it's obvious the child has very little dress sense. The Prince likes his guests to be *chic, soignée, haut ton, les derniers cris* . . .
HILDA. Quite right, young man. Cinderella would make a laughing-stock of the whole family. Certainly she must stay at home and fill our hot-water bottles.
CINDERELLA (*tearfully*) Must I really?
HARDUP (*to Cinderella*) There, love, never mind! You can watch the ball on Fairyvision, when I've mackled it up a bit.
DANDINI (*giving Hardup an invitation*) Your invitation, Baron. And now I really must dash along to Magical Mansions. See you all tonight, then? Ten o'clock, remember—don't be late!

(DANDINI *sweeps out, with a parting sniff at the weeping* CINDERELLA, *who is comforted by* BUTTONS)

TILDA (*dancing*) Hooway, hooway! Tilda's going to dance with Pwincie!
HILDA. Silence, Tilda! This rejoicing is premature. The question now is, what are we going to wear?
TILDA. New dwesses! We must have lovely new dwesses an' wings and things an' buttons and bows!
HILDA. Exactly! And I know how to get them. (*She goes to the jar containing money*)
HARDUP. Nay, lass, that's mortgage money for landlord!
CINDERELLA. Hilda, you mustn't take that! Squire Rudolf will be coming for it at any moment!
HILDA. Nonsense! We're only going to invest it. Come along, Tilda.
TILDA. Are we going to buy dwesses from the Magic Shop?
HILDA. What, from that little fairy round the corner? Of course not! We're going to Madame Norma.*
TILDA. Oo, goodie!
HARDUP. Hold on! Suppose Squire comes and turns us out of house and home?
HILDA. What do I care? When the Prince sees me he'll offer me a suite in the Palace!
BUTTONS. A sweet in the Palace—and I only get a coughdrop in the kitchen!

(HILDA *and* TILDA *exit* R)

CINDERELLA. It's too bad! Nobody takes any notice of me— and all because I haven't any proper clothes.

* The name of a local house may be substituted.

Scene 3 THE STORY OF CINDERELLA 17

HARDUP. Never mind, lass, come and help your dad to weed the pumpkin patch. Buttons-me-lad, isn't it about time you began cooking dinner?

(HARDUP *and* CINDERELLA *exit* L)

BUTTONS. Dinner! I haven't washed up the breakfast things yet. Let's hope the Baron's patent washing-machine doesn't want a bit o' macklin'.

(*He switches on the washing-machine. The hands begin to move*)

Good! Something's working at last!

(BUTTONS *puts the pots in the sink and the hands begin to wash them. He takes groceries from Cinderella's basket and dashes up and down the kitchen unit opening doors and discovering improbable objects*)

Now I'll put the dinner on. Can't beat these modern kitchens for saving time and energy. A place for everything and everything somewhere else! For instance here's the frying unit—no, it's the boot-blacking unit! Ah, this is it—you just put the chops in here and . . .

(*A rod flies out with the washing attached*)

No, that's the drying unit! (*He puts the washing back*) Can't think why some people are satisfied with the old-fashioned kitchen range—on the go from morning to night instead of taking things easily like I do. (*He strains to reach a pile of cartons, which topple over*) Oh dear—all fifty-seven kinds of soapflakes! Won't there be a row if they get in the gravy! (*He pauses to survey the mess*) Somehow my housekeeping never does look like the advertisements! The trouble is I've got too many jobs—in fact, I'm a complete pre-war domestic staff rolled into one.

No. 2a BALLAD (BUTTONS)

I'm the maid-of-all-work and the jack-of-all-trades,
    The butler, the boots, and the Buttons;
All faithful retainers of various grades
    Unite in the person of Buttons:
There are twenty-five bells in the big servants' hall,
With only yours truly to answer them all,
And even in dreamland I still hear the call
    Of "Buttons! Hi, Buttons! Where's Buttons?"

Every bothersome job on each day of the year
    Increases the burden of Buttons,
From cleaning the silver to drawing the beer—
    There's never a drop left for Buttons:

At Christmas I hope for a generous tip;
Deep down in his pocket the Baron will dip
And into my hand he will stealthily slip
   Just buttons, old buttons, brass buttons!

I'm the dressmaker, dairy-maid, daily help too,
   The bailiff, the batman, the Buttons;
Yes, captain and cabin-boy, cookie and crew—
   Behold them before you in Buttons:
If it wasn't for Cinders I'd run right away,
But as long as she needs me beside her I'll stay,
Content when I hear her caressingly say,
   "Poor Buttons! Dear Buttons! My Buttons!"

(CINDERELLA *runs in, agitated*)

CINDERELLA. Oh, Buttons, that dreadful Squire Rudolf's coming down the lane and Hilda's taken the money to pay him! Whatever shall we do?

BUTTONS. Don't worry, Cinders. You leave Squire Rudolf to me.

(*A knock is heard*)

Ah, there he is! Don't be afraid—I'll answer the door.

(*He opens the door* R.
    RUDOLF *enters*)

RUDOLF (*ignoring Buttons*) Ah, delighted to find you at home, Miss Cinderella! I have much to say to you. But business before pleasure! First there's a tiresome little matter to settle with your father.

CINDERELLA. I'm so sorry, but I'm afraid the Baron isn't in.

RUDOLF. Really? That's curious—very curious! As I passed the garden just now I felt sure I saw him diving into the dustbin.

CINDERELLA. Oh, no, that was a man from the Corporation.

RUDOLF. Indeed? Well, it doesn't matter a bit—so long as the Baron's left my little white envelope.

CINDERELLA. I'm afraid I don't understand.

RUDOLF. It's a shame to bother your pretty little head with sordid financial details. But the fact is, today happens to be quarter-day, which means that your father owes me precisely seventy-nine pounds eleven and twopence.

CINDERELLA. Perhaps I'd better be frank. We can't pay you just yet because . . . (*She falters*)

RUDOLF. Because?

CINDERELLA. Because we haven't the money.

RUDOLF. And a very good reason, too! I couldn't think of a better. Awkward, isn't it?

CINDERELLA. Very.

SCENE 3   THE STORY OF CINDERELLA   19

RUDOLF. Well, I don't want to be unreasonable. Suppose you just hand over the seventy-nine pounds eleven, and we won't say any more about the twopence?
BUTTONS (*producing some coins*) Tell you what, here's twopence. Suppose you take that and say no more about the seventy-nine pounds . . .
RUDOLF. A very clever suggestion. But I'm afraid it doesn't quite solve our little problem.
CINDERELLA. I'm so sorry. I quite see this must be very inconvenient.
RUDOLF. Not in the least. You see, now I can do what I've wanted to do for a long, long time.
BUTTONS. And what might that be?
RUDOLF. Don't you see? Now I can foreclose on the estate. Yes, I can turn you out of house and home.
BUTTONS (*aside*) We'll see about that. (*He begins to fiddle with the washing machine*)
CINDERELLA. You couldn't be so cruel!
RUDOLF. Oh, couldn't I?
BUTTONS. Oh, couldn't you?
RUDOLF. Of course, if you'd rather stay on here it *could* be arranged.
CINDERELLA. But how?
RUDOLF. Quite simple. (*Kneeling*) Accept the hand of one who adores you madly!
BUTTONS (*aside*) So that's your game, is it?
CINDERELLA. Marry you? Why, I'd rather starve!
RUDOLF. I'd make you the happiest and richest girl in the Land of Fairytale.
CINDERELLA. The richest, perhaps, but the happiest—never!
RUDOLF. I advise you to think it over, if you don't want to see your poor old father thrown into the gutter.
CINDERELLA. But it would kill father to be parted from his inventions.
RUDOLF. Oh yes, I've heard about those inventions. All built in, aren't they?—and therefore the landlord's property. Mine, all mine!
BUTTONS (*politely*) If you're taking over, sir, perhaps you'd like to see a demonstration of the Hardup patents. (*Aside to Cinderella*) Leave this to me, Cinders—and keep out of the way.
RUDOLF. A very good idea, me boy. Where are they?
BUTTONS. If you'd just step this way, sir, this is the celebrated Hardup Automatikitchen. May I take your hat, sir? Thank you. (*He takes Rudolf's hat and puts it on the sink*) Now here we have the Hardup washing-machine.

(*The hands wash a plate*)

RUDOLF. Very ingenious. (*Coming closer*) How does it work?

BUTTONS (*pulling a lever*) Like this!

(*The hands seize Rudolf by the horns and pulls his face in the basin*)

RUDOLF. Ouch! I'm scalded! I'm drowning!

BUTTONS. Sorry, sir.

(*The hands seize Rudolf by the nose*)

RUDOLF. Ugh! Id's god hold ob by dose!

BUTTONS. Has it really, sir? I'd better turn it off, then. (*Pretending to search*) That's funny! Can't find the switch!

RUDOLF. Ow! Leggo by dose!

BUTTONS (*releasing it*) That better, sir? Now, if you'll just step over here I'll demonstrate the patent mixer.

(*He signals to* CINDERELLA, *who puts dough from a dish into Rudolf's hat*)

The main thing, of course, is to get the quantities right. You just set the dials like this—pull a string—and hey presto—flour, lard, currants, beaten egg . . .

(*He pulls a string attached to overhead cans from which various fluids and powders pour over Rudolf*)

RUDOLF. Ow! Stop it! You're blinding me—choking me—ugh!

(BUTTONS *thrusts a frying-pan into a hand of the washing-machine. As* RUDOLF *backs towards it, the frying-pan whacks him, while the machine's other hand grasps him by his coat*)

RUDOLF. Help! Murder! Police! (*He breaks free at last and staggers towards the Fairyvision set, which, as he touches it, gives him an electric shock*) Ouch! I've been struck by lightning! I'm off—I've had enough!

(*He dashes to the door,* BUTTONS *handing him his hat. At the door he turns, hat in hand, to shake his free fist at the laughing* CINDERELLA *and* BUTTONS)

    My curse on you, audacious lad and miss!
    Think not that you have heard the last of this:
    I shall return—though for the nonce I beat
    An orderly and dignified retreat!

(RUDOLF *puts on his hat and is covered in flour and dough before making a hasty exit.* CINDERELLA *runs into* BUTTON'S *arms and they dance round in jubilation, singing*)

No. 2b REPRISE OF No. 2a (BUTTONS *and* CINDERELLA)

BOTH.   In the up-to-date kitchen each job can be done
        By pressing a couple of buttons;
      For bathing the baby or toasting a bun
        The housewife relies on her buttons:

SCENE 4   THE STORY OF CINDERELLA

BUTTONS. But the only contraption so simple and strong
          That it lasts you a lifetime and never goes wrong
BOTH.   Is the all-purpose gadget that's singing the song
          Of Buttons, young Buttons, just Buttons.

CURTAIN

SCENE 4

SCENE—*The Woodland Glade.*

When the CURTAIN *rises,* RUDOLF *is discovered on a soap-box addressing a meeting of* FAIRIES. *Beside him is a banner with the scrawled legend "Double Pay for Overtime".*

RUDOLPH. So, One for All and All for One,
          O members of the Union
          Of Gnomes and Fairies, Elves and Sprites!
          Prepare to stand upon your rights
          And press your just demands, becos
          Miss Mabel Mabb, your greedy boss,
          Grows fat upon your sweat and skill!
          So, follow my advice!
FAIRIES.   We will!
RUDOLF.   That's splendid! Carried unopposed!
          I now declare this meeting closed.
          (*He prepares to leave with the banner*)
          Comrades, farewell! (*Aside*) Me dark design
          Succeeds! The maiden shall be mine!

   (RUDOLF *exits.*
   FAIRY FAY *enters with a cauldron*)

FAIRY FAY. Look out, you loafers! Here's Miss Mabb, M.A.;
            From now on there'll be no more time for play.
            Come, lend a hand to get this cauldron ready!
            Let's put it over here. Be careful! Steady!

   (*Helped by other* FAIRIES, *she prepares the cauldron and lights the fire beneath.*
         MISS MABB *bustles in ringing a little bell. She might have a broomstick-powered cycle*)

MISS MABB. Now, no more talking—can't you hear the bell?
            I want no slackers in *my* fairy dell!
            Come, rally round—there's lots of work to do!
            Some volunteers, please—you and you and you!
            Our full resources we must now deploy
            That little Cinderella may enjoy

Herself this evening at the Palace ball
And be no more the drudge of Hardup Hall.
She needs a glamorous exclusive gown,
A coach-and-six to take her up to town.
With your assistance I can raise a spell
To furnish these and other things as well.
So to your places! Form a fairy ring
And in the bubbling pot prepare to fling
Th'ingredients of our magical collation
As I shall name 'em in my incantation!

(*During the following Incantation, the* FAIRIES *dance round the cauldron, throwing in the ingredients and stirring as requested*)

MISS MABB. Page of parish magazine
Edited by Rural Dean;
Unattractive local view
Framed in purple *passe-partout*;
Ear of soccer referee—
Rash and ill-advised was he
Once too often to declare
Fair was foul and foul was fair!
Take a ladle, stir the lot
In the arty-crafty pot;
Don't forget to spice the brew
With a tube of liquid glue;
Sealing-wax and candlewick
Make the gruel slab and thick—
Make it thick and make it slab
By the art of Mabel Mabb!

FAIRIES. Making cauldrons boil and bubble
Takes a deal of toil and trouble!

MISS MABB. Lucky semi-precious stone,
Pinch of pheno-barbitone,
Plastic bag and Woolworth ring
In the murky mixture fling;
Add a dose of castor-oil,
Bring it gently to the boil;
Speech of prominent M.P.
Broadcast by the B.B.C.—
What could make a dryer fuel
For to cook the gruesome gruel?
Now the pricking of my thumb
Tells it's time to skim the scum,
Bottle, seal and clearly label,
"Made and Sold by Maison Mabel."

FAIRIES. Though our pay is miserable,
We obey behest of Mabel!

SCENE 4   THE STORY OF CINDERELLA

MISS MABB.	Thanks, elves and fairies! Now the charm's wound up.
	Skim well, and cool it in a loving-cup.
	You'd be surprised what wonders it reveals
	When taken half-an-hour after meals.
	(*Confidentially to the Audience*)
	Oh, by the way, if anyone
	Would like to know just how it's done
	They'll find the simple recipe
	Fully described in Chapter Three
	Of my new book about bewitchin'
	Called, "Magic in the Modern Kitchen".
	Astound your friends, amaze relations,
	With Mabb's ingenious incantations.
	Order your copy—don't forget—
	From the attendants—ninepence nett.
1ST FAIRY.	O proud employer, not so fast!
	This potent magic will not last
	Without our service and goodwill—
	Be sure that you command them still!
	Already we have toiled all day
	So, meet our claim for double pay
	For labour after midnight hour
	Or we abate this magic power!
FAIRIES.	Yes, we abate this magic power!
MISS MABB.	What, double pay? I never heard
	Of such a thing!
1ST FAIRY.	One further word.
	If to these terms you won't agree
	When midnight strikes—then so shall we.
FAIRIES.	Double pay for overtime,
	Or upon the midnight chime
	Down at once our wands we lay.
	Grant us therefore double pay—
	Double pay for double trouble
	Or we prick the magic bubble!
MISS MABB.	I can't afford to pay you double!
	Fairies, think! Be reasonable!
	To go on strike would be a crime!
FAIRIES.	Double pay for overtime!
MISS MABB.	The stubborn fact I must repeat—
	This monstrous claim I cannot meet!
1ST FAIRY.	Miss Mabb, this attitude's unwise.
	Although we deeply sympathize
	With Cinderella, in our view
	We ask no more than is our due,
	And though we'll try to keep awake

      And on the job for Cinders' sake,
      Promptly at twelve o'clock midnight
      Each fairy wand will dim its light,
      And Cinderella, coach and all
      Must bid farewell to Prince and ball!
MISS MABB. So be it, then! Too well I know my hands
      Are powerless without your fairy wands.
      Herein I see fell Rudolf's handiwork!
      'Twas he who taught my loyal staff to shirk.
      Yet Cinderella still shall have her chance—
      The Prince shall claim her for the supper-dance.
      Who knows? One glorious crowded hour may bring
      A royal lover and a wedding-ring!

        CURTAIN

        SCENE 5

SCENE—*The Kitchen of Hardup Hall. Evening.*

When the CURTAIN *rises,* HILDA *and* TILDA *are discovered dressing for the ball.* TILDA *is sitting in front of the washing-machine, whose hands are drying her hair with a towel.* BARON HARDUP *and* BUTTONS *are struggling to encase the* HON. HILDA *in her corsets.* CINDERELLA *is holding a tape-measure round her waist, calling out its diminishing circumference as* HARDUP *gradually tightens the corsets.*

HILDA. Tighter! Tighter! What is it now?
CINDERELLA. Fifty-one—fifty-and-three-quarters—fifty-and-a-half—fifty-and-a-quarter . . .
HILDA. Won't do! Tighter, tighter!
HARDUP. Talk about a quart in a pint pot! Hold on, lass—only wants a bit o' macklin'.

(*He fetches a huge spanner, which he operates in the small of her back. Appropriate ratchet noises. The corset tightens quickly*)

CINDERELLA. Forty-nine, forty-eight, forty-seven . . .
HILDA. Ow! Stop! You've contracted my kidneys and deflated my diaphragm!
CINDERELLA. Forty-six, forty-five.
HARDUP. That'll do, that'll do. By rights it's a welder's job.
TILDA. Cindewella! Cindewella, come and make it wub harder!
HILDA. Stay where you are, Cinders, and fasten my shoes. At this rate we shall never get to the ball.
TILDA. It isn't dwying pwoperly! Instead of glamouwous twesses I'll have wows of dwaggly waggletails!

Scene 5   THE STORY OF CINDERELLA

BUTTONS. Soon fix that!

(*He touches a switch. The hands towel vigorously*)

TILDA. Ow! It's putting its fingers in my eyes!

(BUTTONS *switches off.*
Meanwhile CINDERELLA and HARDUP help HILDA on with her dress. CINDERELLA comforts TILDA and arranges her hair. HILDA takes mincing steps in evidently tight shoes*)

HILDA (*rehearsing*) Ai quaite agree, your Royal Highness! If it's all the same to your Royal Haighness, Ai think it would be much naicer if we sat this one out! (*She trips up and falls on her bustle, dragging HARDUP with her*)

TILDA. Do huwwy up, Hilda, or we shall be dweadfully late!

HARDUP (*picking himself up*) Plenty o' time! Still, I'd better go and get the Atommycar started. It *may*—mind you I don't say it will—but it *may* want a bit o' macklin'.

(HARDUP *goes out* L. CINDERELLA *helps* HILDA *and* TILDA *on with Edwardian-style motoring kit—bonnets, veils, scarves and goggles*)

HILDA. If only we didn't have to travel in Father's dreadful home-made Atommycar!

BUTTONS. What's wrong with the Atommycar? One of the Baron's greatest inventions—purrs like a kitten!

(*A horrible clanging noise is heard outside. It is the Atommycar starting up*)

HILDA. A kitten indeed! More like tomcats in the dustbin!

TILDA. Isn't it thwilling to think we're weally going to dance with the Pwince?

HILDA. What a hope you've got! You'll be lucky if you get Mr Dandini in the Paul Jones.

(TILDA *begins to wail*)

CINDERELLA (*to Hilda*) Now look what you've done! Cheer up, Tilda. Hilda was only joking.

TILDA. Oh, no, she wasn't! She's always sowing the seeds of fwustwation in my sub-conscious!

(HARDUP *enters in motoring-cap, muffler and goggles*)

HARDUP. Now then, lasses, stop fratchin'. The Atommycar's running sweet as a gramophone record.

HILDA. Yes—after the first movement you turn over.

HARDUP. Nay, she'll get you to the Palace in no time. Come on—mustn't keep his Royal Highness waiting!

HILDA. Now, Cinderella, remember what I told you. As soon

as we've gone you can tidy up, fill the hot-water bottles, cut some sandwiches, make some hot soup, brew some coffee . . .
BUTTONS. I could just do with a sandwich and a cup of coffee.
HILDA. Not for you, you rude boy. Nor for you, either, Cinderella. Of course there'll be a banquet at the Palace, but after the drive home we shall be simply ravenous. Do you understand?
CINDERELLA. I understand, Hilda. And I hope you enjoy yourself as much as you deserve.
HILDA. I fully intend to. Good night!
TILDA. Good night, Cinders. We'll tell you all about the Pwince.

(HILDA *and* TILDA *go out* R)

HARDUP. Good night, lass! (*Kissing her*) Eh, it's a pity you're not coming! I've half a mind to . . .
CINDERELLA (*eagerly*) Yes, Father?
HILDA (*off*) Father, we're late!
HARDUP. Some other time, lass—some other time!
HILDA }
TILDA } (*off; calling*) Father!

(*The* BARON *goes out* R. CINDERELLA *and* BUTTONS *run to the door and wave. A series of explosions indicates the departure of the Atommycar.* CINDERELLA *turns away to hide her tears.* BUTTONS *rubs his hands in satisfaction*)

BUTTONS. Well, if we can't go to the ball at least we've got Hardup Hall to ourselves for a change. Eh, Cinders?
CINDERELLA. Yes, I suppose we have. But—I did so want to see the Prince.
BUTTONS. Never mind, we'll see him on FV.
CINDERELLA. Yes—but he won't see me. And a good job, too, while I'm looking like this.
BUTTONS. But, Cinders, you look wonderful. Always do.
CINDERELLA. Do you really think so, Buttons?
BUTTONS. Course I do! Now I tell you what, first I'll go and feed my tame lizards and the Baron's white mice. Then we'll switch on FV and see how the family's getting on at the Palace. (*He goes to the lamp*)
CINDERELLA. Yes, do that, Buttons dear. No, don't light the lamp—I'd rather sit here in the firelight.
BUTTONS. Right-ho. I shan't be long—and keep your chin up.

(BUTTONS *exits* L)

CINDERELLA. Dear old Buttons! He's so kind—and I *think* he's a teeny bit in love with me. I wouldn't hurt his feelings for the world—but why doesn't he realize that if I can't dance with the Prince I'd much rather be alone among the cinders, like the poor little Cinderella that I am.

Scene 5   THE STORY OF CINDERELLA

No. 3 SONG (CINDERELLA)

I'm only Cind'rella—forgotten Cind'rella,
    So homely and shabby and shy;
Neglected Cind'rella, forsaken Cind'rella,
    Unlucky Cind'rella am I!

Like poor Polly Flinders, I sit among cinders
    And never go out on the spree;
I've no time to dally at pictures or Palais,
    And boys never whistle at me.

I've chilblains and blisters, and two selfish sisters—
    No wonder I'm sick of it all;
I wish I were pretty and well-groomed and witty
    And going tonight to the ball!

But I'm only Cind'rella—forgotten Cind'rella,
    Who's trying so hard not to cry;
Neglected Cind'rella, forsaken Cind'rella,
    Despairing Cind'rella am I!

(MISS MABB *enters* R *as the song finishes. She is seen as a dim, cloaked figure*)

MISS MABB. Cinderella! Cinderella!

CINDERELLA. Who's that?

MISS MABB. Only I, Cinderella. Only your godmother who wishes you well.

CINDERELLA. My godmother? I didn't know I had one.

MISS MABB. Of course you have, child. A godmother who loves you as dearly as she loved your real mother, who died so long ago.

CINDERELLA. Did you really know my mother?

MISS MABB. Indeed I did! And very beautiful she was—nearly as beautiful as you yourself, my dear.

CINDERELLA. Now you're making fun of me! I'm not at all beautiful—at least, only Buttons thinks so.

MISS MABB. Nonsense! Why, child, you have only to look in the glass!

(*She hands* CINDERELLA *a mirror*)

CINDERELLA (*looking into it*) But—this isn't me! This is—why, surely she must be a princess! That beautiful necklace—that coronet!

MISS MABB. Never mind her jewels, child. Look at her face. When your eyes sparkle—as they do now—so do hers. When you smile—as you do now—she smiles back.

CINDERELLA. Why, so she does! (*Repeating slowly*) So—she—does! But—that is what *her* lips are saying!

Miss Mabb. Because her lips are yours. Her smile is yours. Her eyes—her heart—her hopes and dreams—they are all yours, my child.
Cinderella. But her jewels—her lovely dress . . .
Miss Mabb. Are the reflection of your own wishes. Of wishes that shall be granted this very night, if you do as I tell you.
Cinderella. Then—this is a magic mirror?
Miss Mabb. It is.
Cinderella. And you are . . . ?
Miss Mabb. Don't you know me, child?
Cinderella. I seem to know your voice. Won't you come into the firelight so that I can see your face?

(Miss Mabb *does so*)

Why—it's only the little Fairy Round-the-Corner!

(Miss Mabb *throws off her cloak, revealing splendid fairy robes. There is now no trace of her former eccentricity*)

Oh! Please forgive me—I didn't know . . .
Miss Mabb. Of course you didn't, child. How could you? To you I was a frumpish little old lady who had been so long away from Fairyland that all its magic had faded. But like other exiles, on special occasions I still wear my national costume. And this is a very special occasion. Tonight, my dearest godchild, I am going to send you to the ball at the Palace Beautiful, where you will dance with Prince Charming.
Cinderella. To the Ball—to dance with the Prince! Why, that's the dream of my heart! But how is it to come true?
Miss Mabb. That is easier than you think. Give me the mirror, child! (*She takes it and rubs it*) As I came by I noticed a fine pumpkin-patch in the kitchen garden.

(Buttons *comes in, pausing at the door to stare at Miss Mabb*)

Ah, just in time, young man! Won't you oblige your young mistress by digging up a pumpkin—the biggest you can find?
Cinderella. Don't be shy, Buttons. This is Miss Mabb, my fairy godmother who's come to take me to the ball.
Miss Mabb. And while you're about it, young man, I wonder if the Hardup livestock includes half a dozen mice and a nice plump rat?
Buttons. That it does, mum. The Baron breeds mice for their whiskers, and there's a rat in the trap.
Miss Mabb. Excellent! Now, the only other things we need are six intelligent lizards.
Buttons. Your luck's in, mum. I keep lizards for pets.
Miss Mabb. Such affectation! Go and fetch them at once, there's a good boy. Run along, now.

SCENE 5   THE STORY OF CINDERELLA

(BUTTONS *hesitates*)

CINDERELLA. Please do what she tells you, Buttons.

BUTTONS. All right, Cinders, if you say so. But mind you, I wouldn't let *any*body muck about with my lizards.

(BUTTONS *exits.*

During the following Invocation, FAIRIES *enter in a graceful ballet, carrying Cinderella's ball dress, etc. They are headed by* FAIRY FAY, *who carries a goblet which she hands to* CINDERELLA. *As she drinks the* FAIRIES *close round her*)

MISS MABB.   Fairies, hither at my call,
Bringing joy to Hardup Hall;
Let your brightness banish gloom
From this dark and dingy room;
Lo, the wonder-working cup!
Cinderella, drink it up!
As the goblet touches lip
From your heart shall sorrow slip,
Rags and homespun drab and drear
Shall dissolve and disappear;
In their place shall now be seen
Silken gown to grace a queen,
Necklace bright with gold and gem,
Coruscating diadem:
Nature, thus improved by Art,
Soon shall win a royal heart.
Now the mirror answers true;
You are she, and she is you.

(*At the close of the Invocation the* FAIRIES *part, revealing* CINDERELLA *in all her splendour.* FAIRY FAY *passes her the mirror*)

CINDERELLA (*looking in the glass, then down at her dress*) It's true, then! Now I have everything—except a pair of shoes. (*To* Miss *Mabb*) Doesn't your magic run to that?

MISS MABB. It would if it had to, but it doesn't. (*She produces a pair of glass slippers*) These are no magic slippers, but the very pair I wore at my own first ball. Take them, my child—and may they bring you as much happiness as they brought me.

CINDERELLA (*taking the slippers and putting them on*) Why, they're made of glass! How lovely! And they fit perfectly—what a good thing we both take twos!

(BUTTONS *enters* L *with mice, rat, lizards and pumpkin on a tray. He pauses at the door to stare in amazement.*

The FAIRIES *withdraw*)

BUTTONS. Why, what's happened? Who's this lady? And where's Cinders? What have you done with her, you old . . . ?

CINDERELLA. Hush, Buttons! Dear Buttons, don't you know me?
BUTTONS. Cinders, is it really you? Why, you're a princess!
CINDERELLA. Of course I'm not! I'm just the same inside, really, only now I'm happy because I'm going to the ball.
BUTTONS. But how will you get there?
MISS MABB. Leave that to me. Ah, I see you've brought the pets and the pumpkin. Put them over here.

(BUTTONS *does so*)

Let me see—(*touching each in turn with the wand*) pumpkin, rat, mice, lizards—good! (*She waves her wand over them*)
   Fly away Peter and fly away Paul,
   Fair Cinderella is off to the ball!

(*The pumpkin, etc., vanish with effect. A painted balloon makes a good disappearing pumpkin*)

BUTTONS. Why, where have they gone?
MISS MABB. Look!

(*A coach-and-six appears on the FV screen*)

BUTTONS. Well I'm blowed! Where did that lot come from?
MISS MABB. It is your pumpkin—now Cinderella's coach. It is your six mice—now six horses. It is your big fat rat—now a big, fat coachman. It is your six intelligent lizards—now six intelligent footmen.

(*The coach fades*)

BUTTONS (*going to the door*) Here, hold on! Suppose it's a trick? (*He opens the door*) No, there's the coach all right enough! (*Turning back*) All the same, how do I know I'm not dreaming?
CINDERELLA. Why, Buttons, aren't I real enough?
BUTTONS. You aren't as real as you were, miss, and that's a fact. There, now I'm calling you miss instead of Cinders. See what I mean?
CINDERELLA. Couldn't Buttons go to the ball, too?
BUTTONS (*eagerly*) That's an idea! (*A doubt strikes him*) What as?
CINDERELLA (*to Miss Mabb*) I thought—perhaps he could be an extra footman.
MISS MABB. It could be arranged.
BUTTONS (*covering disappointment with indignation*) What, me hobnob with Alf and Fred? Not likely!
MISS MABB. And who are Alf and Fred?
BUTTONS. My best lizards.
MISS MABB. So you don't wish to accompany them?
BUTTONS. Not me! I'd much rather spend a nice quiet evening filling in my pools.

CINDERELLA (*piqued*) Please yourself, of course. (*To Miss Mabb*) When do we start?

MISS MABB. Very soon, my child. But first, mark this solemn warning. My power ceases on the last stroke of midnight. Precisely at that moment you will once more be the ragged little girl I found by the fireside. Your coach will again be a common pumpkin, and your staff will leave the servants' hall for pets' corner.

BUTTONS. And jolly glad I shall be to see Alf and Fred again.

(*The door opens, with light shining through it. The sound of hooves is heard*)

MISS MABB. Listen, the horses are growing impatient.

CINDERELLA. And so am I!

MISS MABB. Then off you go, child—but remember you must leave Prince and Palace before the clock strikes twelve.

CINDERELLA. I'll remember. But what about you, Miss Mabb? Are you staying, or can I drop you anywhere?

MISS MABB. That's very kind of you, my dear. Yes, I'd welcome a lift back to the Magic Shop—I'm getting too old for broomsticks. Let me help you with your train. (*She does so*)

CINDERELLA. Please, let's hurry!

MISS MABB. One moment, child. Aren't you going to say thank you to Buttons? I couldn't have done all this without him, you know.

BUTTONS. No, I bet you couldn't!

CINDERELLA. Forgive me, Buttons dear. I hadn't really forgotten you.

BUTTONS. No, miss, 'course you hadn't. Enjoy yourself—and remember to come back at twelve sharp like the lady says.

CINDERELLA. Of course I will. Good-bye, Buttons—and thank you so much.

(*She kisses her hand to* BUTTONS, *and throws him a rose from her breast. He catches it. She calls out of the door*)

All right, coachman! Cinderella's coming to the ball!

CINDERELLA *and* MISS MABB *go out.* BUTTONS *raises the rose to his lips while the refrain of his song is softly played. The* CURTAIN *falls, rising immediately on* BUTTONS *waving from the door, with Cinderella's rose prominent in a jam-jar on a shelf.*

CURTAIN

ACT II

Scene 1

SCENE—*The Road to the Palace.*
This is played in front of TABS. *There is a signpost with arms reading* "TO THE PALACE" *and* "TO HARDUP HALL", *and a milestone.*

When the CURTAIN *rises, the Atommycar, a home-made Emmett-style vehicle, has broken down and* BARON HARDUP *is trying to mend it. His tools are scattered around, and* HILDA *is watching.* TILDA *is sitting on a milestone, taking off her shoes and rubbing her feet.*

HILDA. I said this would happen. But no-one ever listens to me. Why, we should have done better with British Road Services.
TILDA. Or even Bwitish Wailways!
HARDUP. Now don't whittle! I'll have her straining at the lead in a couple o' shakes! Only wants a bit o' macklin'.
TILDA. Why can't we wadio for a taxi?
HARDUP. Where's your pride, lass, where's your pride? Go to the Palace in a common taxi when we've got our own supercharged fluorescent hydrostatic double dynamic Atommycar?
HILDA. Atommy-rot!
HARDUP. I like that! Let me tell you, this here Atommycar splits an atom once every ten seconds. That's what makes it go—when it does go.
HILDA. Then why isn't it going now? Are the atoms unusually tough?
HARDUP (*pouring dried peas from a can into his hand*) Now that's just it. Look at 'em—nothing like the atoms you used to get pre-war.
TILDA (*weeping*) We'll be late—I know we will!

(*Car clatter effect is made by percussion*)

HILDA. What on earth's that?
HARDUP. Nowt that can't be put right. Watch me!

(*He attacks the engine of the Atommycar with his tools. The clatter effect continues pianissimo to the rhythm of the following Number*)

No. 4 PATTER TRIO (BARON HARDUP, HILDA *and* TILDA)
HARDUP.
    If you can hear a bumpin' an' a creakin' an' a crack-a-lin'
    It only means Atommycar requires a bit o' mack-a-lin';

Scene I   THE STORY OF CINDERELLA

Perhaps she's got a nasty chill upon her carburettor
An' a dose of liquid paraffin will quickly make her better:
Yes, she'll purr just like a pussy if you only treat her gently—
She'll be sweeter than a Cadillac an' better than a Bentley:
If you give me half a minute I'll discover what's the matter
An' I'll stop this most peculiar an' irritatin' clatter!

HILDA.   Such an irritating clatter!
TILDA.   Such a nasty howwid clatter!
ALL.
   Yes, I'll/he'll stop this most infernal and infuriating clatter!
HILDA.
   It really is degrading for the Honourable Hilda
   To be stranded with the Baron and his second daughter
      Tilda—
   A predicament I find particularly aggravating
   When a banquet is preparing and a royal prince is waiting
   With his eligible noblemen uncritically amorous,
   And *Tatler* representatives all ready with their cameras,
   But golden opportunities you'll very quickly shatter
   If you don't cure that contraption of its diabolic clatter!
HARDUP.   Natter, natter, natter, natter!
HILDA.   Yes, our chances you will shatter!
HARDUP
HILDA *and* TILDA } (*together*)
   Nay, I'll soon cure this } contraption of its diabolic clatter!
   If you don't cure that
TILDA.
   I know you both despise me and you think I'm just a silly
   But an accident like this is vewy bad for ickle Tillie;
   Yes, it wobs me of my self-wespect and makes me feel in-
      fewior;
   It gives me sinking feelings in my sensitive intewior;
   I'm jumpy as a gwasshopper and colder than an icicle—
   I wish I'd had the commonsense to bowwow Button's
      bicycle—
   My nerves are all to pieces and my heart's a pitter-patter
   And I'll shortly have hystewics if you cannot stop the
      clatter!
HARDUP.   Nay, there's really nowt the matter!
HILDA.   Then why can't you stop the clatter?
HARDUP
HILDA *and* TILDA } (*together; banging the engine with a spanner*)
   That'll stop the miserable an' infuriatin' clatter!
   Stop the most abominable and infuriating clatter!

(*The clatter ceases*)

HARDUP. There, I told you that'd stop it!
HILDA. It may have stopped the noise but it hasn't started the

car. I don't know about you, Tilda, but I'm going to thumb a lift.

TILDA. Oo, goodie! Look, here's a Wolls—and a lovely boy dwiving! Come on—pwetend we're back in the A.T.S.!

(*Sound effect of passing car.* HILDA *and* TILDA *mime thumbing a lift as the car passes in front of the stage from* L *to* R *without slowing down. Winning smiles, anxiety, disappointment, tears from* TILDA. *Meanwhile* HARDUP *has coaxed a few grunts and splutters from the Atommycar*)

HILDA. Did you see that?
TILDA. Nasty wude man!
HILDA. Cut us dead!
TILDA. And lots of woom in the back seat!
HILDA. Never mind, here's a Bentley!
TILDA. So thewe is! Hooway! And another lovely boy!
HILDA. Well, if you don't at first succeed . . .
TILDA. Twy, twy again! Bags I the seat next the dwiver!

(*They mime as before, but this time the car evidently stops off stage* L)

HILDA. Look, he's slowing down!
TILDA. He's stopped!
HILDA. He's getting out!
TILDA. He's looking at us! (*Waving*) Oo-oo!

(*Simpering and waving, they walk towards the car, then stop short*)

HILDA. He's turning away!
TILDA. He's getting in again!
HILDA. He's starting up!
TILDA. He's dwiving off! Boo-hoo!
HILDA. Poor man—something wrong with his eyesight! Fancy not recognizing the Honourable Hilda Hardup!

(*The Atommycar begins to make a series of more or less regular splutters*)

HARDUP. There you are—told you I'd mackle her up! Come on, lasses—all aboard for the Palace Beautiful!

(*They all get into the Atommycar. The splutters swell to a roar, then suddenly cease*)

This is where we came in.

(TILDA *wails*)

You hold your noise.

HILDA (*getting out*) I suppose this means we'll have to walk?

(TILDA *wails more loudly*)

Come on, you! (*She pulls* TILDA *out*)

Hardup. Hold on! One of you girls got a safety-pin?
Hilda. What good would that do?
Tilda. Aren't the atoms splitting pwoperly?
Hardup. I don't know about the atoms, but my trousers are.

(Tilda *suddenly begins to wave and jump*)

Hilda. Disgusting! (*To Tilda*) And what's the matter with you?
Tilda. Something's coming!

(*The* Baron *produces a telescope and peers through it*)

Hilda. Another car?
Hardup. Nay, lass, it's a coach-and-six—grand as owt like the Coronation!
Tilda. Make it stop, Daddie! Tell it to give us a lift!
Hilda. Can you see who's inside?
Hardup. Not rightly, lass—wait a minute! Why, it's a beautiful lady—must be a princess!
Tilda. Yes, I can see her now. Oo, isn't she lovely!
Hilda. Princess or no princess, I'm going to ask her for a lift.
Hardup. You'll have a job, lass. Them horses have got wings.
Hilda. Never!
Hardup. They have an' all! Coach has taken off—it's airborne—it's climbing steady!
Tilda. He's wight! Look!

(Cinderella's *coach, drawn by winged horses, passes overhead.* Hardup *follows it with his telescope, while* Hilda *and* Tilda *vainly try to thumb a lift. The coach effect can be arranged by a model or shadowgraph, seen in perspective against the backcloth*)

Curtain

Scene 2

Scene—*The Ballroom of the Palace.*
Up c *there is a dais with steps up to it. There are entrances to it up* r *and* l. *On the dais is a large clock with movable hands, now set at 10.30. The clock must be low enough to enable Rudolf to reach it. On the clock is a figure of Father Time. There are large double doors* l *leading to the banqueting hall. A throne is set* rc *facing* l.

When the Curtain *rises, the* Guests *are discovered dancing.*

No. 5 GAVOTTE (Guests)

Dandini *is moving about officiously, carrying a wand.* Prince Charming *enters* l. *He is wearing a modern dressing-gown and watches the scene in dazed surprise.* DANDINI *sees him and hurries forward in alarm. The music stops, the* GUESTS *applaud and chat in groups.*

DANDINI. Your Royal Highness!
PRINCE. Dandini, who are all these people? And why are they making such a noise?
DANDINI. But these are the guests of your Royal Highness!
PRINCE. Guests! Nonsense! I'm not having a party, I'm having a night off.
DANDINI. Softly, softly, your Highness! It would never do for your Highness to be recognized like this.
PRINCE. Like what?
DANDINI. Like—like Mr Noel Coward in his wilder days.
PRINCE. Rubbish, I'm perfectly respectable! Besides, if a Prince can't relax in his own Palace, where can he relax?
DANDINI. But not tonight, sir—not tonight, please! Simply everybody's here—including the Press!
PRINCE. Then get them out, man—get them out!
DANDINI. I really don't see how I can do that, sir!
PRINCE. Then I will! (*He moves forward*)
DANDINI (*hastily covering him*) All right, sir—you win! (*To the guests*) Ladies and gentlemen, the bar is now open!

(*The* GUESTS *all hurry through the double doors*)

PRINCE. That's better. Now perhaps you'll explain what all this is about.
DANDINI. The fact is, sir, we thought your Royal Highness needed cheering up. So we decided to throw a party ..
PRINCE. In my name, without my consent—and on my day off! Really, Dandini, you have a nerve!
DANDINI. But, sir, we did it for the best. We've invited all the loveliest girls in the Land of Fairytale.
PRINCE. Looks like a bus-load from Butlin's. And I suppose I'm expected to pick the Beauty Queen?
DANDINI. Well, since your Highness mentions it, we thought a beauty competition would lend rather a novel touch . . .
PRINCE. Now look here, Dandini—get this straight. I'd planned to spend this evening in bed with a detective story. For two pins I'd go straight back there.
DANDINI. Oh no, your Royal Highness, please don't! Whatever would the gossip-writers say?
PRINCE. All right! I'll go and dress and in ten minutes I'll look in.
DANDINI. Your Royal Highness is ever his people's slave.
PRINCE. But not yours! Mind, I only said I'd look in! I won't make a speech.
DANDINI. Your Highness!

Scene 2   THE STORY OF CINDERELLA   37

PRINCE. I won't judge a beauty contest.
DANDINI. Sir!
PRINCE. And on no account will I make an exhibition of myself on the dancing-floor! Understand?
DANDINI. But, sir, the loveliest girls in the Land of Fairytale...
PRINCE (*striding off*) They're all yours, Dandini—all yours!

(*The* PRINCE *exits*)

DANDINI. Oh dear! And I thought H.R.H. would be so pleased! Whatever shall I tell the Press? Still, there's one consolation—as the Prince doesn't want any girls I shall have first pick!

(RUDOLF *enters dressed as a footman and wearing a not impenetrable disguise*)

RUDOLF. Mr Dandini, I believe!
DANDINI. Hello? I suppose you're the extra footman from *Universal Aunts*?
RUDOLF. Correct.
DANDINI. Are you familiar with the duties of waiter?
RUDOLF. I know well enough how to wait——
DANDINI. Good!
RUDOLF (*heavily aside*) —for a thing I want.
DANDINI. Then later on you can help the wine steward. Meanwhile you'd better stand at the door and announce the guests.
RUDOLF. Very good. (*Aside*) A splendid chance to spot Cinderella! But shall I recognize her in her new finery? Oh yes—there's no mistaking a home perm! (*He stands at the top of the staircase beside the entrance*)

(*The ball* GUESTS *return, carrying glasses*)

DANDINI. My lords, ladies and gentlemen! I have to announce that his Royal Highness the Prince Charming will shortly honour you with his presence.

(*Cheers*)

Unhappily his doctors have forbidden him to make his usual speech of welcome.

(*General disappointment*)

They have also forbidden him to display his unrivalled skill on the dancing floor.

(*Groans*)

However, his Royal Highness has graciously appointed me as his deputy. Ladies fortunate enough to attract my notice will receive a parchment certifying they have danced with a prince by proxy. And now, ladies and gentlemen, on with the dance!

(*Applause. There is a gavotte or other dance. During the next speech, various* GUESTS *enter*)

RUDOLF (*announcing new arrivals*) Sir Richard and Lady Whittington. Mr Jack Horner. Her Royal Highness the Princess Scherazade. Madam Hubbard and Miss Muffet. His Royal Highness the Prince Charming.

(*The dance stops.*
   PRINCE CHARMING, *now in court dress, enters and hurries straight to his throne without glancing round. Murmurs of sympathy as the* GUESTS *part to make way for him. As he passes they bow and curtsy. He lounges on the throne and produces a detective novel, which he begins to read, entirely ignoring the company. Music and dancing are resumed*)

(*Announcing at intervals*) His Excellency Ali Baba. Mr and Mrs Jack Spratt. Miss Goldilocks.

(*Before joining in the dance, these* GUESTS *bow or curtsy before the* PRINCE, *who takes no notice. The dance ends*)

The Lady Cendrillon.

   (CINDERELLA *enters.* RUDOLF *makes no sign of recognition. Murmurs of admiration. All the men surge about her; the women discuss her behind fans. Still the* PRINCE *takes no notice. The music recommences and* DANDINI *asks* CINDERELLA *to dance. He leads her on to the floor. The* PRINCE *looks up, drops his book and rises. Everyone pauses and stares at him. He strides across the floor, thrusts* DANDINI *aside and bows to Cinderella*)

PRINCE. Out of the way, Dandini! (*To Cinderella*) Lady Cendrillon, Dandini here told me that tonight I should meet the loveliest girl in the Land of Fairytale. I did not believe him; he has broken that promise too often. Now I owe—to Dandini, an apology; and to you, this homage.

   (*He kisses her hand. Applause*)

DANDINI. A miraculous recovery!

PRINCE. But how is it we have never met before? Tell me, Dandini, where did you find her?

DANDINI. Well, sir, the fact is that until today she was bound by enchantment.

   (*General sensation*)

PRINCE. Really?

DANDINI. Yes, sir. You see it was like this.

No. 6 TRIO (DANDINI, PRINCE *and* RUDOLF)
(Repeat of No. 3)

DANDINI.
   The Lady Cendrillon, surpassing Cendrillon,
      She lived in a cave by the sea;

SCENE 2   THE STORY OF CINDERELLA

>   Bewitching Cendrillon, enchanted Cendrillon,
>   A beautiful mermaid was she!
>
>   Enchantments they bound her, till Dandini found her,
>   Close guarded by dolphin and whale;
>   But soon he released her—a process which pleased her
>   For that was the end of her tale!

PRINCE.
>   O lovely Cendrillon, attractive Cendrillon,
>   This story sounds fishy, I fear!

DANDINI (*aside; to* Cinderella)
>   O please don't deny it—I'm sure that he'll buy it
>   If only you say so, my dear!

(*The* PRINCE *laughs and waves* DANDINI *aside*)

RUDOLF (*aside*)
>   That lady's perfection, to my recollection,
>   Is shared by but one other wench!
>   Now who can she be, yonder Lady Cendrillon?—
>   Why, that's Cinderella in French!

(RUDOLF *retires triumphantly. The Trio tune is repeated in waltz time, the* PRINCE *and* CINDERELLA *leading the dancing to it. The dance ends with applause*)

PRINCE.   A toast, a toast to Beauty's eyes!
>   And while we lift the leaping bubbles,
>   As lightly may our spirits rise,
>   As quickly vanish all our troubles!

(RUDOLF *brings on a tray with glasses of sparkling wine to the Prince and Cinderella.* CINDERELLA *takes a glass, recognizes Rudolf, drops the glass and runs into the* PRINCE'S *arms.*

     RUDOLF *retires with a Mephistophelean laugh.* DANDINI *ushers the whispering* GUESTS *into the banqueting hall while the* PRINCE *soothes* CINDERELLA.

     The PRINCE *and* CINDERELLA *exit into the banqueting hall. The* LIGHTS *fade. The clock-face is spotlit while the hands move to 11.40. The* LIGHTS *come up.*

     HILDA *and* TILDA *enter* R, *dusty and bedraggled. They sit on the steps and take off their shoes*)

TILDA. I *said* we should have wadioed for a taxi. Oo, my chilblains!

HILDA. Never mind your chilblains. What about my varicose veins? (*She stands up. There is a creaking noise*) Ow! I'm too stiff to stand up and too sore to sit down.

(BARON HARDUP *strides in, swinging his arms. His trousers are slung over his shoulder like a hiker's knapsack, and his short pants make admirable shorts. He marches briskly round the room*)

HARDUP. Well, lasses, here we are at Palace! Ee, I feel all the better for a bit of a stroll!
HILDA. So you call seven leagues a bit of a stroll, do you?
HARDUP. Mind you, I won't deny it's made me a bit sharp-set. Eh, I could do with a plate of hot-pot! (*Sniffing*) Am I dreaming, or is something cooking?

(*An* ATTENDANT *enters up* L *carrying a tray with covers. He goes towards the banqueting hall*)

TILDA (*sniffing*) Oo, lovely gwavy!
HILDA (*sniffing*) Delicious dumplings! Must be the supper interval.
HARDUP (*pointing*) Meet the Bisto Kids. (*To the attendant*) Eh, young feller! Young feller!
ATTENDANT (*disdainfully*) This is the Palace Beautiful. You should have turned right for the Youth Hostel.

(*He goes through the doors, which close in Hardup's face*)

HILDA. It *is* the supper interval! Come on, Tilda—here's something to cure your chilblains!

(DANDINI *enters from the banqueting hall*)

DANDINI. Ah, good evening, Baron. So sorry you're late. I'm afraid supper's off.

(RUDOLF *enters wearing an opera cloak and Italianate moustachios*)

HARDUP. Off? What, not even fish-and-chips.
DANDINI. So sorry, but we're not frying tonight.
HARDUP. Well, I don't know what country's coming to!
RUDOLF. What is all zees? No supper for il barone and ze beautiful signori? Neffair mind—il Conte Rudolfo 'e feex! (*He flourishes a banknote*)
HILDA. Count Wudolfo? Why, he weminds me of Squire Wudolf!
HILDA. Certainly a striking likeness.
RUDOLF. Ah, zat is my cousin—ze black sheep of ze family! I am 'ead of ze Eetalian branch.
TILDA. Fancy, a bwanch manager!
RUDOLF. And now we all go into supper, no? (*He gives the note to Dandini*)
DANDINI. That will be quite all right, sir. Glad to fix you up at any time.
RUDOLF (*taking Tilda's arm*) Zees way!

(DANDINI *opens the doors of the banqueting hall.*
RUDOLF, HARDUP *and* HILDA *exit.* DANDINI *comes down* C)

DANDINI. Hooray—another ten bob the income-tax man doesn't know about! (*He adds the note to his bank-roll, which he pockets*) Oh yes, this is just the job for me. Plenty of fun, plenty of tips and no Pay-As-You-Earn.

No. 7 SONG (DANDINI)

The harder you labour today,
    Tra la,
The less in proportion you earn,
The higher the tax you must pay,
    Tra la,
The Government takes it away,
    Tra la,
And what do you get in return?
Yes, what do you get in return?
  But chaps who are crafty and boys who are wide
  Are quietly making a bit on the side:
    Tra la la la la,
    Tra la la la la,
We're making a bit on the side.
    Tra la la, etc.

My tip it will pay you to take,
    Tra la,
Yes, take all the tips that you can!
It's the little bit extra you make,
    Tra la,
That helps you to fiddle and fake,
    Tra la,
And diddle the income-tax man,
That overworked income-tax man.
  Why bother the chap with each petty amount
  That percolates into your private account?
    Tra la la la la ,
    Tra la la la la,
Your flourishing private account.

(*He slaps his pocket*)
    Tra la la, etc.

(DANDINI *exits into the banqueting hall.*
RUDOLF *enters* L)

RUDOLF. At last the witching hour draws nigh!
    O what a clever demon I!
    As midnight spreads her mantle sable,
    In this disguise impenetrable
    Miss Mabb's match-making scheme I'll spoil,
    Her plans confound, her purpose foil!
    'Tis simply done! Back, warning finger!
    (*He puts back the hands of the clock to 11.30*)

Entice the lovesick lass to linger
Until the belfry's brazen tongue
With dreary ding and doleful dong
Announces in a tone doom-laden,
"Too long you've loitered, luckless maiden!"
Then instantly all elfin hands
Shall dim their lamps and down their wands;
Then Cinderella, all unwary,
Shall lose at once her splendours faery,
Her Prince, her hopes of ring and throne—
And then shall Rudolf claim his own!

(TILDA *enters* L)

TILDA. Oo-oo! I see you!

RUDOLF (*aside*) Confound her! Did she detect me, I wonder? Ah no! I am secure, me plot's afoot!

TILDA (*waving*) Oo-oo! Wudy! It's Tillie!

RUDOLF (*still aside*) But perhaps I had better humour her— the poor fool's in love with me and will believe anything I tell her. (*To Tilda*) And what can I 'ave ze pleasure of doing for ze beautiful signora?

TILDA. I was afwaid you'd awwanged to meet another girl under the clock.

RUDOLF (*forgetting his accent*) Under the clock? (*He shivers guiltily, then recovers*) I mean—under ze clock?

TILDA. Well, that's where I found you just now.

RUDOLF. Ah! But I only put my watch right by ze clock, no?

TILDA. It looked to me as if you were putting ze clock wight by your watch, yes?

RUDOLF. I assure ze signora zat she maka bigga mistake. Ze time 'e go so fast wiz ze bella signora, my watch 'e not catch up.

TILDA (*skittishly*) How many girls have you told that to? I bet you're a wegular Don Juan!

RUDOLF. Ah! Don Giovanni! (*He sings*) "*La ci darem la mano, La mi dirai di si.*"*

TILDA. Twust you to know that music always weleases my inhibitions! Come on, let's find a nice quiet seat under a potted palm and you can tell me the stawy of *Il Twovatowe*.

RUDOLF (*singing as he leads* TILDA *off*) "*Ai nostri palm-tree ritorneremo, l'antica pace, ivi godremo.*"*

(RUDOLF *and* TILDA *exit up stage.*
CINDERELLA *enters from the banqueting hall*)

CINDERELLA.
The Prince has eyes and ears for none but me:
O yes, he loves me—that is plain to see!

---

* These operatic fragments are better known as "Give me thy hand, O fairest" and "Home to our mountains".

The trouble is, he hasn't said so yet:
Perhaps it isn't royal etiquette
To start proposing at half past eleven
To a girl you didn't even know at seven.
There's no Miss Mabb to tell me what to do,
So, Father Time, I must appeal to you.

No. 8 BALLAD (CINDERELLA)
(*This Number is an apostrophe to the figure of Time on the clock*)

O Father Time, forbear
  To tell the moments fleet;
Pray take an easy chair
  And rest your weary feet!
For one brief hour, delay
  Your dread accountancy
Until my love shall say,
  "O marry, marry me,
  (Hey-derry-down
  White wedding-gown)
  O marry, marry me,
  And here forever stay!"

Ah, heed my tender song;
  Allow no midnight bell
With too-impatient tongue
  My maiden hopes to knell!
O send me not away
  Until at last I hear
My royal lover say,
  "I love you, dearest dear,
  (Hey-ding-a-ding,
  Bright wedding ring)
  I love you, dearest dear;
  With me forever stay!"

(PRINCE CHARMING *enters* L)

PRINCE. So here you are, Lady Cendrillon! Thank heaven I've found you again!

CINDERELLA. Your Royal Highness talks as if we had been parted for an eternity instead of only five minutes.

PRINCE. To me, every hour spent with you is a moment. Every moment without you is a thousand years.

CINDERELLA. Really? Then next time we meet you'll be quite an elderly gentleman.

PRINCE. Next time? Why wait until then? Lady Cendrillon, need we ever part?

CINDERELLA (*aside*) This is it! (*To the Prince*) I'm afraid we must —for tonight at least.

PRINCE. Then what are you doing for lunch tomorrow? Oh bother, I've just remembered—I'm lunching with one of my Ministers.
CINDERELLA. Oh? Where?
PRINCE. That depends. The Minister of the Interior prefers the *Hotel Splendide.**
CINDERELLA. So do I.
PRINCE. But the Chancellor of the Exchequer insists on the *Miss Muffet Milk Bar.**
CINDERELLA. I see.
PRINCE. But couldn't we meet for tea?
CINDERELLA. Perhaps. But I'm afraid your Royal Highness might not recognize me.
PRINCE. Not recognize you? Why, Cendrillon, I should know you anywhere!
CINDERELLA. And—anyhow?
PRINCE. Of course—even if you were dressed in rags!
CINDERELLA. I wonder! (*Aside*) Why doesn't he come to the point?
PRINCE. Won't you promise to meet me?
CINDERELLA. I really don't think I ought to, your Royal Highness. After all, we hardly know each other.
PRINCE. Cendrillon, how can you be so cruel! Why, I feel that I've known you all my life! When I look into your eyes I feel . . .
CINDERELLA. Go on.
PRINCE. Hang it, how can I possibly tell you what I feel!
CINDRELLA. At least you can try.
PRINCE. Cendrillon, don't you realize that I'm asking you—begging you——
CINDERELLA (*aside*) At last!
PRINCE. —imploring you to be my . . .

(DANDINI *enters followed by* BARON HARDUP, HILDA *and* TILDA)

DANDINI. Your Royal Highness, allow me to present the eminent inventor, Baron Hardup and his two daughters.

(*During this, other* GUESTS *enter from the banqueting hall. Among them is* RUDOLF)

PRINCE. Confound you, Dandini!
HARDUP (*shaking hands with the Prince*) Pleased to meet your Royal Highness. Nice palace you've got.
PRINCE (*stiffly*) I'm glad you think so, Baron.
HARDUP. Mind you, I don't say it couldn't do with a bit o' macklin'.
DANDINI. The Honourable Hilda Hardup and Miss Tilda Hardup.

* Local establishments may be substituted.

(HILDA *and* TILDA *curtsy awkwardly. The* PRINCE *bows*)

CINDERELLA (*aside*) Of all people—oh, it's too bad! (*Looking at the clock*) And only another twenty minutes!

DANDINI. Ladies and gentlemen, pray take your partners for the waltz.

PRINCE (*aside to Cinderella*) Cendrillon, with all these people about I can't say what I was going to say. But when this dance is over we'll go out on to the balcony.

CINDERELLA. But there won't be time! I promised Miss Mabb—I mean, I promised my mother I'd leave by midnight.

PRINCE. But it's only twenty to twelve. The dance will be over by then—and I'll see you to your coach myself.

CINDERELLA. Will you really? Oh, that will be lovely!

(*Waltz. The* PRINCE *dances with* CINDERELLA, *and* DANDINI *is grabbed by* HILDA)

RUDOLF (*aside*) Laugh and dance, my lady gay!
    Clasp your prince while yet you may!
    As you twirl and glide about
    Swift the sands are running out!
    Dance, for little do you know
    That the palace dial is slow;
    Won't you get a nasty shock
    When you find it's twelve o'clock!

TILDA. Come on, Count Wudy—welease my inhibitions!

(RUDOLF *dances with* TILDA, *whirling her giddily around. Twelve o'clock begins to strike. At the first stroke* CINDERELLA *stops in alarm, the Prince looking at her anxiously. The other dancers pause and stare.* RUDOLF *casts off* TILDA, *who continues to twirl dizzily until she slides to the floor*)

RUDOLF (*counting the strokes*) One! Two! Three! (*Etc.*)

CINDERELLA. Hark! What's that? Surely it can't be . . . ?

PRINCE (*looking at his watch*) Twelve o'clock already? Why, the Palace clock must be slow!

(CINDERELLA *runs to the door.*
    RUDOLF, *still counting, bars her way*)

Now how did that . . . ? (*Missing Cinderella*) Cendrillon, where are you?

(CINDERELLA *runs towards the banqueting hall. Confusion.* CINDERELLA *passes into the banqueting hall unnoticed by the* PRINCE, *just before the last stroke sounds*)

RUDOLF (*counting*) Twelve.
    (*Aside*) There it goes—the final stroke!
        Toiling fairies, cast your yoke!

Magic rainment rich and rare,
Melt in dew, dissolve in air!
Rags and tatters, reappear!
Clothe again me pretty dear!

(CINDERELLA, *once more in rags, runs blindly out of the banqueting hall*)

PRINCE. Cendrillon! Cendrillon! Where is my Cendrillon!

(CINDERELLA *collides with him. He catches hold of her*)

Why, you little ragamuffin, what are you doing in my palace?

(CINDERELLA *breaks free and escapes, with the* PRINCE, DANDINI *and* GUESTS *in pursuit.* RUDOLF *laughs in evil triumph*)

CURTAIN

SCENE 3

SCENE—*The Woodland Glade.
It is moonlight, and snowing.*

When the CURTAIN *rises,* CINDERELLA *enters, distressed.*

CINDERELLA.
Alas, I'm lost, and cannot tell at all
Which winding pathway leads to Hardup Hall!
O for a friendly face, a hand to guide me!
If only faithful Buttons were beside me!

(*There is the sound of an aircraft humming*)

Hark! What is that? What eerie murmur loud?
(*Peering*)
What little speck that grows against the cloud?
Ah, now a moonbeam banishes the gloom
Revealing—Buttons flying on a broom!
(*Waving*)
Hi, Buttons, help! Your Cinderella's stranded!
Hooray, he's seen me!

(*A crash; off*)

Goodness—he's crash-landed!

(BUTTONS *enters* R. *He is rubbing himself and pulling a broom on which a cushion has been tied*)

CINDERELLA (*embracing him*) Buttons, darling Buttons, I'm so

Scene 3 THE STORY OF CINDERELLA 47

glad to see you! However did you find me? Have you hurt yourself? Where did you get that magic broom?
  BUTTONS. Saw you on FV. O.K., except for a bump and a lump. (*Indicating the broom*) Obligingly left by Miss Mabb when you gave her that lift.
  CINDERELLA. Does it still work?
  BUTTONS. 'Course it does! Old-fashioned but hard-wearing. Get you home in no time.
  CINDERELLA. But—will there be room for us both?
  BUTTONS. Of course, if you ride pillion. Look, I've fixed you up a nice cushion. (*He bestrides the broom*)
  CINDERELLA. How thoughtful! (*She gets on behind him*)
  BUTTONS. Now, catch hold of my waist—tight as you like—that's the ticket! Comfy?
  CINDERELLA. Oh, very! But—I've never ridden pillion on a broomstick before. I'm going to shut my eyes.
  BUTTONS. Nothing to the Big Wheel at Blackpool!
  CINDERELLA. It's the take-off that scares me. I shall feel safer up in the clouds.
  BUTTONS (*masterful*) None of that! You've been up in the clouds long enough—high time you came down to earth.
  CINDERELLA (*sighing*) I suppose you're right. Fancy—the Prince didn't even know me in my rags!
  BUTTONS. Never you mind him—*I'm* taking care of you now! Come on, fasten your safety-belt. This glade'll make a first-rate runway.
  CINDERELLA. Dear Buttons, I feel so safe with you!

  (*They go out* L *astride the broom. There is the noise of a take-off and flight.*)
    TILDA *enters* R)

  TILDA (*calling*) Oo-oo! Oo-oo! Wudy, Wudy, whewever are you? It's Tillie, poor ickle Tillie out in the cold, cold snow! (*With a change of tone*) Might as well save my bweath, I suppose! I bet he's with the other men—all looking for that Lady Cendwillon! And why? 'Cos she's a foweigner! Yes, it's the same evewywhewe—nobody looks at you these days till you pwetend you're fweely adapted fwom the Fwench!

  (*A slipper falls from the sky*)

Oo, that's a big snowflake! Why, it's a slipper—a glass slipper—dwopped fwom the sky!

  (RUDOLF, *now undisguised, enters and steals up behind her*)

  RUDOLF (*snatching the slipper*)
    What have we here? A valuable clue!
    The little lady's scintillating shoe!

TILDA. Wudy, Wudy, give it back! It's mine—I found it first!
Why, it isn't Count Wudy at all—it's Squire Wudolf!
RUDOLF.
    I must have dropped me whiskers in the snow!
    You like-a my Eetalian cousin, no?
TILDA. Well, of all the mean twicks to play! (*Brightening*) But
I can still call you Wudy, can't I?
RUDOLF.
    You'd better be advised and hold your tongue
    Or you won't call me anything for long:
    Out of me way—I'm after bigger game.
TILDA.
    You monster! But I love you just the same!
RUDOLF (*peering* R)
    Hark! Voices! Someone's rapidly approaching!
    The Prince himself—on my preserve encroaching!
    Seek on, good sir, throughout this woodland shady—
    Look where you will, you'll never find the lady;
    For I alone possess the shining key
    To your beloved's true identity!
TILDA (*snatching the slipper*)
    Oh, no, you don't!
RUDOLF.   How dare you? Give it back!
TILDA.
    Shan't! (*She throws the slipper off* R) That'll put the Pwince
        upon her twack!
    Hooway, he's got it! (*To Rudolf*) Now you'll have to be
        Content to make the best of ickle me!
RUDOLF.
    Confound you, superannuated miss!
    Come here—I'll have the life of you for this!

(TILDA *runs off* L, *screaming*)

    Just now I'm far too busy to pursue her,
    But later at me leisure I'll undo her!

(RUDOLF *exits* R)

No. 9 CHORUS SONG (MISS MABB *and* FAIRY FAY)

(MISS MABB *and* FAIRY FAY *enter* L, *carrying sacks. They mime to the tune.* MISS MABB *begins the 1st verse,* FAIRY FAY *repeating the chorus in a thin, tuneless voice*)

MISS MABB. Though I'm getting far too old for wonder-working–
FAIRY FAY.   Wonder-working
MISS MABB. Though I'm past the lovely April of my prime—
FAIRY FAY.   Of her prime,

Miss Mabb. Since my disaffected staff are prone to shirking—
Fairy Fay.   Prone to shirking—
Miss Mabb. Stop, stop! (*To Fairy Fay*) Who asked you to embroder my D'Oyley Carte?
Fairy Fay. Sorry, Miss Mabb. I must have got the wrong key.
Miss Mabb. All *your* keys are rusty. Never mind, suppose we ask the children to help us out! Do you hear that, children? No need to learn the words—you just repeat the end of each line as loudly as you can. Remember, I said *loudly*!

(*During the Song* Fairy Fay *leads the Audience in the chorus*)

Miss Mabb. Though I'm getting far too old for wonder-working—
All.   Wonder-working,
Miss Mabb. Though I'm past the lovely April of my prime—
All.   Of her prime,
Miss Mabb. Since my disaffected staff are prone to shirking—
All.   Prone to shirking,
Miss Mabb. I have to do a little overtime—
All.   Overtime!
Miss Mabb. I've come to finish off an incantation—
All.   Incantation,
Miss Mabb. To add a sack of toadstools to my store—
All.   To her store,
Miss Mabb. But I grieve to say this modern generation—
All.   Generation,
Miss Mabb. Simply won't believe in magic any more!
           Ah!
     No, they don't believe in magic any more,
                         Any more,
     No, they don't believe in magic any more!
All.   Ah!
     No, they don't believe in magic, etc.
Miss Mabb. I've broom for fairy broomsticks—you can fly 'em!
All.   You can fly 'em!
Miss Mabb. There's a tandem model made to carry two—
All.   Carry two,
Miss Mabb. I've powerful potations—won't you try 'em?
All.   Won't you try 'em?
Miss Mabb. And pints of health-promoting honey-dew—
All.   Honey-dew:
Miss Mabb. I've a potted caterpillar preparation—
All.   Preparation,
Miss Mabb. That your disappearing hair will soon restore—
All.   Soon restore,
Miss Mabb. But a public that has no imagination—
All.   'Magination,
Miss Mabb. Simply won't believe in magic any more.
All.   Ah!

　　　　　　No, they don't believe in magic any more,
　　　　　　　　　　　　　　　　　　　　Any more,
　　　　　　No, they don't believe in magic any more!
Miss Mabb. Though your most devoted friend will never tell you
All. 　　　　　　　　　　　　　　　　　　Never tell you,
Miss Mabb. Why it is that all alone you sit and sigh—
All. 　　　　　　　　　　　　　　　　　　Sit and sigh,
Miss Mabb. An amazing remedy I'll gladly sell you—
All. 　　　　　　　　　　　　　　　　　　Gladly sell you,
Miss Mabb. The shilling jar contains a week's supply—
All. 　　　　　　　　　　　　　　　　　　Week's supply:
Miss Mabb. But I'd better seek some other occupation—
All. 　　　　　　　　　　　　　　　　　　Occupation,
Miss Mabb. Discredited my ancient faery lore—
All. 　　　　　　　　　　　　　　　　　　Faery lore,
Miss Mabb. For the people of this modern generation—
All. 　　　　　　　　　　　　　　　　　　Generation,
Miss Mabb. Simply won't believe in magic any more.
All. 　　　Ah!
　　　　　　No, they don't believe in magic any more,
　　　　　　　　　　　　　　　　　　　　Any more,
　　　　　　No, they don't believe in magic any more,
　　　　　　　　　　　　　　　　　　　　Any more!

(Miss Mabb *and* Fairy Fay *exit* L.
Rudolf *enters* R)

Rudolf. I'll make that interfering Tilda rue it!
　　　　The Prince has found the slipper where she threw it;
　　　　But soft, he's drawing nigh! Behind a tree
　　　　I'll hide meself and see what I can see!

(Rudolf *exits* L.
　The Prince *and* Dandini *enter* R. *The* Prince *is carrying a slipper*)

Prince. Yes, it is hers, Dandini—hers, I say!
　　　　My darling must have lately passed this way!
　　　　Why, such a slipper did I never see on
　　　　The foot of any lady but Cendrillon!
　　　　See how the crystal shines beneath the moon!
Dandini. Be sure, your Highness, we will find her soon:
　　　　Hidden, disguised, bewitched though she may be
　　　　Her whereabouts cannot be kept from me!
　(*Aside*) Said he, with confidence he's far from feeling,
　　　　His apprehension tactfully concealing.
Prince. Thanks for these cheering words, Dandini, I
　　　　On your expert assistance will rely!
　　　　Away with you, the country to explore
　　　　Castle to cottage! Knock at every door;

>   Neglect no unfrequented avenue;
>   Summon each lady, bid her doff her shoe
>   And try the slipper on, for whomsoever
>   It fits shall be my queen and love forever!

(*The* PRINCE *exits* L)

DANDINI. The job sounds tedious and never-ending—
>   But still, no worse than vacuum-cleaner-vending!

(DANDINI *exits* R.
    RUDOLF *enters* L)

RUDOLF. Aha! Their precious plan I overheard:
>   I listened hard and didn't miss a word!
>   'Tis well! I will away to Hardup Hall,
>   The dandified Dandini to forestall!

(RUDOLF *exits* R)

CURTAIN

SCENE 4

SCENE—*The Kitchen of Hardup Hall. Next morning.*

When the CURTAIN *rises,* CINDERELLA *is preparing mustard foot-baths.* BUTTONS *is anxiously peeping into the cupboards. There are a medicine-bottle and glasses on the sink-unit, also two trays with coffee-cups, tumblers, etc. There is a slipper on one of the stools down* R.

BUTTONS. Now where did I put that pie? (*He opens a cupboard door*) Ah, here we are! (*He takes out a top-hat*) No, it's the Baron's topper! Funny—I know I popped it in somewhere!

CINDERELLA. Never mind about your pie, Buttons—they don't want any breakfast today. They've all got indigestion and bad colds.

BUTTONS. No wonder, after last night's goings-on!

CINDERELLA. Do you know, Buttons, I can hardly believe it all really happened—going to the ball, and dancing with the Prince.

BUTTONS. And me coming to the rescue!

CINDERELLA. But—did we really do all those things? Or was it just a dream?

BUTTONS. A dream? Not on your sweet life it wasn't! Why, there's the slipper to prove it!

CINDERELLA (*picking up the slipper*) So there is—lovely, adorable glass slipper. What a pity I lost the other one! I'm sure I had it when you found me.

BUTTONS. Sure to turn up somewhere—like this pie of mine.

CINDERELLA. Oh, do stop nattering about your precious pie! What about the aspirins and the black coffee and the alka-elzer?

BUTTONS. All ready.
CINDERELLA. Then come on, let's take them up to father and the girls. (*She picks up the coffee tray*) And when they come down we'll give them a nice hot mustard bath.
BUTTONS. And some nasty cold medicine!

(BUTTONS *and* CINDERELLA *go out* L *with the trays.* RUDOLF *climbs in through the window*)

RUDOLF (*sniffing*)
    Ah, breakfast time! A tempting smell of kipper!
    (*He picks up the slipper*)
    What's this? Why, Cinderella's other slipper!
    This pretty thing me purpose will confound
    Unless I hide it where it can't be found;
    Therefore the tell-tale I'll conceal—but where?
    No time to lose—already on the stair
    I hear the footstep of me pretty dear.
    Wherever can I put it? Ah!—in here!
    (*He puts the slipper in a unit compartment*)
    And now I'll knock upon the door and tell a
    Plausible lie to little Cinderella!

(*He goes out by the door* R, *closes it and knocks on it.* CINDRELLA *runs in* L)

CINDERELLA. Now who can this be? I do hope it's the doctor.

(*She opens the door.* RUDOLF *sweeps in*)

RUDOLF. Ah, good morning, Miss Cinderella! I must say you don't seem very pleased to see me.
CINDERELLA. Really, Squire, after what happened at our last meeting you can hardly expect to put out flags.
RUDOLF. Ah, now that's just what I've called to see you about. Miss Cinderella, I want to offer me sincere and heartfelt apologies for me ungentlemanly conduct.
CINDERELLA. That's all very well, you know, but you can't expect me to forgive you just like that.
RUDOLF. I know it's a lot to ask.
CINDERELLA. It certainly is. Still, if you're *really* sorry . . .
RUDOLF. Oh, I am!
CINDERELLA. Then we'll say no more about it.
RUDOLF. Won't we? Now that *is* a relief? Do you know, I couldn't sleep last night for thinking about you.
CINDERELLA. I don't suppose any of us got much sleep after the ball.
RUDOLF. The ball? What ball?
CINDERELLA. The ball at the Palace Beautiful, of course. Why, you were there yourself!

RUDOLF. Me? Oh, no! I'm not a dancing man.
CINDERELLA. But I saw you there!
RUDOLF. How could you, when neither of us went?
CINDERELLA. Of course we did!
RUDOLF. But when I came to apologize last night I peeped through the window and saw you asleep by the fire.
CINDERELLA. Asleep?
RUDOLF. Fast asleep. I didn't want to disturb you so I went back home and had a nice cup of cocoa.
CINDERELLA. But—what time was this?
RUDOLF. About half past ten.
CINDERELLA. But by then I was on my way to the ball in my coach!
RUDOLF. Your coach? I didn't know you had one.
CINDERELLA. I didn't have—but my Fairy Godmother made me one out of a pumpkin.
RUDOLF. A pumpkin? (*He bursts out laughing*)
CINDERELLA. Why are you laughing?
RUDOLF. Whoever heard of a coach made out of a pumpkin?
CINDERELLA. Are you accusing me of telling fibs?
RUDOLF. Shall we say that you've made rather a silly mistake?
Come, my dear—surely you don't *really* believe that you went to that ball?
CINDERELLA. But I did—I know I did!
RUDOLF. And I'm positive you didn't! Now don't look so upset—the explanation's quite simple. Listen to me!

          No. 10 DUET (CINDERELLA *and* RUDOLF)

RUDOLF.   Weary little maid who should have been **abed**,
               (This is the tale of little Cinderella)
            Airy-fairy fancies in her pretty head,
                 Gaily a-teeming O!
                    While she sat a-dozing
                    By the fire reposing
                  She fell a-dreaming O!
CINDERELLA. Sir, your explanation will not do at all,
             (No sleepy-head is little Cinderella)
          Clearly I remember dancing at the ball,
               Jewels a-gleaming O!
                 Charitable fairy
                 Was no vision airy;
             You are just a-scheming O!
RUDOLF.   If you don't believe me, ask your own **Papa**,
             (Truly I tell you, little Cinderella)
          Coach and coronet and Fairy Godmama,
               So solid-seeming O!
               All, without a question,

                    Due to indigestion—
                    You *were* a-dreaming O!
CINDERELLA. In prevarication pray do not persist,
              (Belle of the ball was little Cinderella!)
              I only tell my dreams to my psycho-analyst;
                    You're just a-faking O!
                    Still you can't deceive me,
                    For I am, believe me,
                    Very wide-a-waking O!
RUDOLF.   You're much mistaking O!

(BUTTONS *enters* L)

BUTTONS. Hello, what's he doing here?
RUDOLF. Ah, Buttons, my young friend!
BUTTONS. Ah, Rudolf, my old enemy!
CINDERELLA. Buttons, what do you think? He says I never went to the ball—that it was just a dream!
BUTTONS. A dream? Well, of all the cheek! Haven't we got the slipper to prove it was real?
CINDERELLA. Why, of course we have! And here it is—(*she misses the slipper*) oh!
BUTTONS. Here it isn't!
CINDERELLA. But I'm sure I put it here! You saw it, Buttons, didn't you?
BUTTONS (*to Rudolf*) Look here, have you pinched it?
RUDOLF. I? What an insulting suggestion!
CINDERELLA. No, he couldn't have—I've been here ever since he came in. Oh, Buttons, I can't help wondering if he isn't right! All those marvellous things simply couldn't have happened to me!
BUTTONS. But they did—I saw them!
CINDERELLA. Perhaps *you* were dreaming, too.
BUTTONS. But how could we both have the same dream?
RUDOLF. Quite simple. You both had the same things for tea, didn't you?
BUTTONS. Well, yes, we did. Toasted muffins.
RUDOLF. There you are!
BUTTONS. But what's that got to do with it?
RUDOLF. Naturally the same muffins gave you both the same kind of indigestion. And, of course, that gave you the same kind of dream.
CINDERELLA. Then I suppose we must have dreamed up the slipper, too?
RUDOLF. Of course. And now you've woken up.
CINDERELLA. I might have known! How could a girl like me ever dance with Prince Charming—except in Dreamland.
RUDOLF. How indeed? Now you youngsters take a tip from your Uncle Rudy and don't mention this to a soul.

CINDERELLA. Of course we won't. Hilda and Tilda would never let us hear the last of it.
RUDOLF. Well, now I really must be getting back to the office. But first, there's just that little matter of the money you owe me.
CINDERELLA. But, Squire, you know we can't pay you!
RUDOLF (*producing a paper*) Ah, ha! Who said anything about paying? All I ask you to do is to sign this.
CINDERELLA (*taking it*) What is it?
BUTTONS. Here, don't sign anything you haven't read through!
CINDERELLA (*reading*) "On behalf of the Baron Hardup, I, his daughter Cinderella——
BUTTONS (*reading over her shoulder*) —do hereby surrender to Squire Rudolf and his heirs for ever——
CINDERELLA. —the old barn in Ditchpond Lane——
BUTTONS. —in full settlement of all moneys owed by me to the said Squire Rudolf——
CINDERELLA. —signed—Cinderella."
RUDOLF. Well, is it a deal?
BUTTONS. Here, what do you want with the old barn?
RUDOLF. Just to do a little private barnstorming.
BUTTONS. What, another amateur dramatic society?
CINDERELLA. But the old barn's only six feet high!
RUDOLF. My acting always raises the roof. Come, what do you say?
CINDERELLA. It's really very generous of you, Squire. The old barn can't be worth more than ten shillings.
RUDOLF. All I desire is your happiness. Sign on the dotted line, there's a good girl. (*To Buttons*) And you witness her signature.
CINDERELLA. But I haven't a pen.
RUDOLF (*offering her one*) Pray accept mine.
BUTTONS. Well, I only hope it's all right.

(BUTTONS *and* CINDERELLA *sign*)

RUDOLF (*aside*) Little does she know that the words "Old Barn" are written in patent vanishing ink. In a few minutes they will disappear. And then—ah, then . . . !
CINDERELLA (*handing back the paper*) Here you are, Squire—all signed and witnessed.
RUDOLF. Splendid! (*Giving her a copy*) And here's a carbon copy for your file.
CINDERELLA. How very thoughtful! I'm afraid I've misjudged you, Squire.
RUDOLF. Yes, haven't you? Well, bye-bye for now. And remember—you can always trust your Uncle Rudy!

(RUDOLF *exits* R. CINDERELLA *waves*)

BUTTONS. I don't know so much about that. There *was* a

strange and beautiful lady at the ball—and she *did* vanish at twelve o'clock. Why, I saw it all on FV!

CINDERELLA. Perhaps I did, too—and then dreamed she was me. Oh well, the sooner I forget about it the better!

(BARON HARDUP, HILDA *and* TILDA *enter* L, *coughing and sneezing.* HARDUP *is wearing a nightshirt,* HILDA *and* TILDA *nightdresses and curlers. They all have dressing-gowns, and slippers on bare feet.* CINDERELLA *pulls the foot-baths forward and pours in boiling water from the kettle*)

BUTTONS. Well, you do look a dickey lot! Never mind—come to Dr Buttons and take your nice meddy-meddy.

(*They grimace, etc.*)

TILDA. Nasty howwid meddy! Tilda wants a chocky.

BUTTONS (*handing round medicine glasses*) You drink it up like a good girl and I'll chuck you a chocky. Come on, now, or I shan't have you on my panel!

(*They line up*)

Are you ready? Get set—one, two, three!

(*They drink the medicine*)

HARDUP. Eh, that was proper nasty!
HILDA. Ugh! It's curdling my vocal chords!
TILDA (*weeping*) Want my chocky! Want my chocky!
BUTTONS (*stuffing a sweet into her mouth*) Here, suck it and shut up.
CINDERELLA. Now come along and have your nice hot mustard baths.

(*They gingerly dip their toes into the foot-baths, and hurriedly withdraw them*)

HARDUP. Ow! It's boiling!
HILDA. It's freezing!
TILDA. It's wetting my tootsies!

(*There is a knock at the door* R)

CINDERELLA (*running to open it*) Oh dear, someone at the door! Not the Squire again, I hope... Why, it's Mr Dandini!

(DANDINI *enters, carrying a slipper*)

TILDA. Oo, and me in my scanties!
DANDINI. Good morning, everybody.
HARDUP. It's nod a good bordig! (*He sneezes*) Choo!
HILDA. And we're not at home.
DANDINI. But this isn't a social call—it's strictly official. I am

seeking an interview with the lady who lost this slipper near the Palace last night.

HARDUP. Why, has lass done a burglary?

DANDINI. She has certainly stolen a very precious object. We have reason to believe she is now in disguise. That's why we're using the slipper to trace her. When she is found it is the intention of his Royal Highness . . .

HILDA. Well, you needn't waste your time on me. Can't you see it isn't my size?

TILDA. Too teeny for Tillie! Nasty thing—take it away!

DANDINI. I was about to explain that it is the intention of his Royal Highness to marry the mysterious lady who has stolen his heart.

HILDA } *(together)* { To make her queen?
TILDA }   { To mawwy her!

DANDINI. Yes, whoever can wear this slipper will certainly wear a crown. However, I see that I needn't detain you . . .

(BUTTONS *looks at the slipper and whispers to* CINDERELLA, *who sadly shakes her head*)

HILDA. Wait, Mr Dandini! Now I look at it, the slipper's just like the one I lost!

TILDA. Let Tillie twy too!

DANDINI. I really don't think . . .

HARDUP. Nay, lad, fair dos! Give lasses a chance!

DANDINI. Very well, go ahead.

HILDA. Me first—I'm eldest! (*She pushes* TILDA *aside and snatches the slipper*) Where's the shoe-horn? Do you hear, Buttons?

(BUTTONS *fetches a tablespoon*. HARDUP *holds* HILDA *while she and* BUTTONS *try to force on the slipper*)

Stop—you've got the wrong foot!

BUTTONS. Why, it's a perfect fit——

HILDA. I knew it!

BUTTONS. —on your big toe!

HILDA. It's not fair—my feet are swollen with walking home!

DANDINI. Next lady, please!

(BUTTONS *tries the slipper on* TILDA)

TILDA (*giggling*) Oo, you're tickling. (*She giggles*) Oo, that was my corn! (*She kicks off the slipper*)

DANDINI (*rescuing it*) Careful—it's made of glass, you know.

TILDA. Yes—magnifying glass! Makes my tootsies look bigger than they weally are.

DANDINI. Sorry, ladies, but it seems we've drawn a blank. Never mind, perhaps your pools will come up this week. And now I must be off—I've a lot of people to interview.

BUTTONS. Here, wait a minute! (*To Cinderella*) Why don't you try, Cinders—I'm sure that slipper's like the one you lost.
HILDA. What impertinence!
DANDINI. I really haven't any time to waste on little girls.
BUTTONS. Why shouldn't she have her chance like the others?

(HARDUP, TILDA, BUTTONS *and* HILDA *begin to sniff, one after the other*)

HILDA. Nonsense! How could she lose the slipper when she didn't even go to the ball?
CINDERELLA (*wistfully*) No, I didn't go to the ball—did I, Mr Dandini?
DANDINI. I should think not, child! Never mind—perhaps you will some day.
HARDUP. Hello, something's burning!
DANDINI (*sniffing*) So there is!
HILDA. Yes, indeed! Fetch the fire-brigade!
TILDA. Oo, lovely smell!
DANDINI. What can it be?
BUTTONS. I know—my pie! (*He rushes to the unit in which Rudolf has put the slipper and extracts a smoking pie, which he begins to scrape*) I knew I'd popped it in somewhere.
HILDA. You careless boy, you!
BUTTONS. Keep your hair on—it'll be lovely when I've scraped it a bit.
DANDINI. It certainly smells good. That reminds me—I haven't had breakfast yet.
BUTTONS. Then try a piece of this. (*He fetches a knife*) Though I says it as shouldn't, I've a light hand with a piecrust. And you'll never guess what's inside.
DANDINI (*taking the knife*) Here, let's see.

(*He cuts the pie. The crust falls off revealing the slipper. General amazement*)

Why, it's another glass slipper! Just like the one I brought!
CINDERELLA (*taking it*) Why, it's mine!
HILDA. Yours? Never!
CINDERELLA. But it is—it is!

(BUTTONS *hands her Dandini's slipper. She puts them both on*)

Look—they both fit me!
HARDUP. Well, I'll be blowed!
CINDERELLA. Buttons, it's true after all! I did go to the ball—I did dance with the Prince—and now it's me he wants to marry—me!

(BUTTONS *turns away to hide his emotion*)

DANDINI. But how did the slipper get into the pie?

CINDERELLA. I can't think, unless . . . Why, of course! Squire Rudolf must have hidden it in the oven! That explains everything!
HILDA. I don't believe it! How could you possibly have gone to the ball in those rags?
CINDERELLA. Surely you remember the Lady Cendrillon?
DANDINI. Lady Cendrillon? But she came in a beautiful coach!
BUTTONS. My pumpkin—with Alf and Fred.
DANDINI. And she wore a silken dress—blazing with jewels!
CINDERELLA. All done by magic—and Miss Mabb.
HILDA. That interfering Little-Fairy-Round-the-Corner!
DANDINI. All very interesting—but it isn't really evidence, you know. We shall require this Mabb person as witness.
CINDERELLA. Then let's go along to the Magic Shop—perhaps she'll change me back into Cendrillon.
HARDUP (*fiddling with the Fairyvision*) Hold on—let's make sure she's in first.
DANDINI. What's that contraption?
HARDUP. My Fairyvision—stop at home and see the world. Here we are—here's Magic Shop.

(MISS MABB *appears on the Fairyvision screen*)

CINDERELLA. And Miss Mabb herself!
DANDINI. Amazing! (*To Miss Mabb*) Good morning, ma'am. I wonder if you can help me . . .
HARDUP. Nay, lad, she can't hear you.
MISS MABB.
 (*To Hardup*) That's all *you* know! Why, certainly I can!
 (*To Dandini*) Good morning! Watch me carefully, young man, While I effect a second transformation.
HARDUP. She's done it! That's Two-Way Communication!
MISS MABB. Remember, Baron, magic holds the clue
To things the Brightest Boy can never do:
But now to work! Come, little Cinderella . . .

(RUDOLF *appears behind her, laughing*)

BUTTONS. Look out!
TILDA. It's Wudy!
HARDUP. Why, the nasty fella!

(*As* MISS MABB *turns the Fairyvision fades out*)

DANDINI. know that man! The police are on his track!
CINDERELLA. Oh, what has happened? Dear Miss Mabb, come back!
HARDUP. No good—she can't—the set's run out o' juice.
DANDINI. Quick—to the Magic Shop—no time to lose!
I recognized the villain's evil face—
A rogue the police are trying hard to trace.

Come on, let's pay an unexpected call
And catch the scoundrel, head and horns and
all!

DANDINI *runs out* R, *followed by* CINDERELLA *and* BUTTONS. *The* BARON, TILDA *and* HILDA *hastily grab their coats, shawls, etc., and follow as—*

the CURTAIN *falls*

SCENE 5

SCENE—*The Way to the Magic Shop.*
(*This short scene can be played in front of* TABS.)

When the CURTAIN *rises*, DANDINI *runs on* R. *He pauses, mops his brow, and produces a paper.*

DANDINI.   Phew! It's no use—I can't keep up this pace!
Let's see the charges Rudolf has to face:
The scoundrel's sure to get it hot and strong;
His catalogue of crime is grave and long—
(*Reading*) "Wanted, for sundry crimes against
    the State:
For buying cigarettes at half past eight,
And treating other reckless gentlemen
To pints of mild-and-bitter after ten;
For criticizing local football teams,
And City Corporation* housing schemes;
For never stamping his insurance card,
And keeping chickens in his own back yard!—
Now, by the sacred name of Libertee,
Such wicked deeds shall not unpunished be!
Press on, Dandini, and you're bound to cop
Rudolf red-handed at the Magic Shop!

(DANDINI *runs off* L. HARDUP *enters* R)

HARDUP.   Eh, what a fuss they make about the Squire!
I haven't time to waste on that old liar—
I'm dashing off to make investigation
Into Miss Mabb's Two-Way Communication—
A scientific problem that defeats me,
And how the old girl does it proper beats me!

(HARDUP *runs off* L. TILDA *runs on* R)

TILDA.   When Wudy was a little demon boy
He had a pitchfork for a Chwistmas toy;

* Loamshire County Council, Blankton Corporation—whatever authority is locally appropriate.

SCENE 5 THE STORY OF CINDERELLA

> One day, by accident, he sat on it:
> That's how his personality was split;
> One half was bent, the other half was busted,
> And even now he's slightly maladjusted.
> You needn't laugh—*you'd* act a little wild
> If you'd sat on a pitchfork when a child!

(TILDA *runs off* L. CINDERELLA *limps on* R)

CINDERELLA. Though at the ball my slippers were all right.
For such a dance as this they're far too tight!
What shall I do? There's still another mile:
I'd better take them off and rest awhile.

(*She takes off her slippers.
The* PRINCE *enters* L)

PRINCE. Hello, where did you come from, pretty lass?—
Here, tell me where you found those shoes of glass?
CINDERELLA. Your Highness, they are mine; by these alone
I know myself, and hope I shall be known.
PRINCE (*recognizing her*)
I know them, too—why, they should surely be on
The little feet of my beloved—Cendrillon!

(*As they embrace,* BUTTONS *enters* R *and stands apart*)

And yet—these rags, I seem to know them, too,
No less than lovely face and twinkling shoe!
CINDERELLA. You should, my love—you saw them once before!
Last time we met, these very rags I wore.
PRINCE. You must be joking!
CINDERELLA. Surely you recall
A ragged child, bewildered at the ball?
PRINCE. Dearest Cendrillon, was it really you?
That little girl? To think I never knew!
Oh then I was distressed, distracted, blind!
Forgive me, dear, for being so unkind.
CINDERELLA. What is there to forgive, since now we two
Are reunited by a lucky shoe!
PRINCE. A shoe that presently behind our carriage
Shall swing to bless a happy royal marriage!
And now my coach, conveniently at hand,
Shall soon convey us to my palace grand
Where jewels are, and many things beside
To grace a lovely and a loving bride!

(*The* PRINCE *leads* CINDERELLA *off* L *with a flourish*)

BUTTONS. Away she goes, without a backward glance!
Of course, I never really stood a chance:

I'd like to run a thousand miles away
And so I would—but there, it's washing-day!

(BUTTONS *exits* R.)

CURTAIN

SCENE 6

SCENE—*The Magic Shop.*

When the CURTAIN *rises,* FAIRY FAY, *indignant, stands beside the open door.* RUDOLF *is laughing behind Miss Mabb, as we saw them on Fairyvision.* MISS MABB *turns and sees him.*

MISS MABB. You? How dare you interrupt my invocation! Miss Fay, I thought I told you I wasn't to be disturbed!

FAIRY FAY. He wouldn't listen. He just barged straight in.

MISS MABB. "Barged", indeed! Not a very fairy-like expression.

FAIRY FAY. It wasn't a very fairy-like action.

MISS MABB. Don't bandy words with me! (*To Rudolf*) As for you, sir, I thought I threw you out yesterday?

RUDOLF. You did! And now it's my turn.

MISS MABB. What do you mean?

RUDOLF (*handing her a paper*) Read this!

MISS MABB (*reading*) "On behalf of the Baron Hardup, I, his daughter Cinderella——

FAIRY FAY (*reading over her shoulder*) —do hereby surrender to Squire Rudolf and his heirs for ever——

MISS MABB. —The Magic Shop . . ." ! No, I can't believe it!

RUDOLF. "Signed—Cinderella!"

FAIRY FAY. So it is!

MISS MABB. But I don't understand! My little shop sold over my head—and to a trade rival! Surely my favourite godchild would never do such a thing! And yet—there's her signature!

FAIRY FAY. Perhaps it's a forgery.

MISS MABB. Would that it were! But too well do I know that hand. How often have I guided Cinderella's infant fingers over her copy-book . . .

RUDOLF. And now she's blotted it!

MISS MABB. That she has! And just as I was about to array her in all the splendour of a peeress at a Coronation!

RUDOLF. Well, from now on you'll have to manage on your spinster's pension. The Magic Shop is mine at last!

MISS MABB (*grabbing her wand*) We'll see about that! Just you wait till I summon my fairy minions!

RUDOLF. You haven't any. They've all signed up with my organization—Magical Monopolies Unlimited.

Scene 6 THE STORY OF CINDERELLA

Miss Mabb. I don't believe it!
Rudolf. Then call them and see!
Miss Mabb. Very well—I will! (*She extends her wand*)
 Elves and fairies, one and all
 Hear your kind employer's call!
 Tell the Demon King that you
 Still to Mabel Mabb are true!
 Elves and fairies, make reply!

(*A pause. Nothing happens*)

 (*Imploringly*)
 Elves and fairies, make reply!
Rudolf. Empty is the silent sky

(Miss Mabb *slowly lowers her wand*)

 Powerless the waning wand
 Drooping from the failing hand:
 Now the reign of Mabb is done,
 That of Rudolf just begun!

Miss Mabb. That it should come to this! Betrayed by Cinderella, deserted by me fairy minions, not a friend in the world...
Fairy Fay (*running forward*) Don't say that, dear Miss Mabb! I will never leave you, never!
Miss Mabb. Why, Miss Fay, I believe you really mean it!
Fairy Fay. Of course I do!
Miss Mabb. Forgive me, child, for ever doubting you! You've always been a comfort ever since I found you under my gooseberry bush.
Rudolf. "There are fairies at the bottom of the garden."
Miss Mabb. Such devotion puts new heart into me! Go and pack our bundles, Miss Fay, and together we will face the world anew!
Fairy Fay. That won't take long—they're such little bundles.

(Fairy Fay *exits* l)

Rudolf. I don't want to be too hard. As it happens, we need a couple of dish-washers in the factory canteen...
Miss Mabb. Do you think we could ever accept a favour from your guilty hand?
Rudolf. But how else can you keep body and wing together?
Miss Mabb. We will shrink from no task, however humble, that will earn an honest crust. If the worst comes to the worst we will even cast horoscopes for the Sunday papers.
Rudolf. Call that honest? Why, only a born idiot would believe such superstitious rubbish!
Miss Mabb. When were *you* born?
Rudolf. December the twenty-third.* Why?

---

* Or opening date of production.

Miss Mabb. A Capricorn subject! Dear me, I'm afraid you're in for a trying week. All the stars are conspiring against you.

Rudolf. I'm accustomed to professional jealousy.

Miss Mabb. Ah, but there's more to it than that. For instance, Tuesday is definitely unfavourable to your financial interests.

Rudolf. Tuesday? But that's today!

Miss Mabb. Quite so!

Rudolf. Of course, I'm not a bit superstitious, really. All the same—would it help if I threw a pinch of salt over my left shoulder?

Miss Mabb. Not in the least! That's just an old wives' tale. On Wednesday——

Rudolf. That's tomorrow!

Miss Mabb. —I predict a crisis in a personal relationship.

Rudolf. Does that mean Cinderella's going to turn me down again?

Miss Mabb. The stars don't go into detail. They're just in a bad mood.

Rudolf. Confound it! Surely I haven't been to all this trouble for nothing? Oh, why didn't I consult Edward Lyndoe!*

(Fairy Fay *runs in with a newspaper*)

Fairy Fay. Saved, saved! Oh, Miss Mabb, we shan't want our bundles after all!

Miss Mabb. Why, what is this?

Fairy Fay (*giving her the paper*) Look, it's all in the paper!

Miss Mabb (*reading*) "Gigantic Swindle Exposed! Panic on Stock Exchange! Magical Monopolies in Liquidation!"

Rudolf. Here, give it me! (*He snatches the paper and reads*) "Factory Looted by Angry Employees!"

Miss Mabb. So *that's* why they didn't answer! Never mind—I forgive 'em!

Rudolf. My lovely factory! But what can the police be doing?

Fairy Fay (*snatching the paper and reading*) "Entire Fairytale Police Force on Nation-wide Hunt for Managing Director."

Rudolf. Why, that's me! So they've found me out!

Miss Mabb. Yes, and now they'll find you in.

Rudolf. Oh, no, they won't! (*He seizes a broom*) With one of these flying brooms I'll soon show 'em a clean pair of cloven hooves!

Miss Mabb. Here, you leave that broom alone! Stop him, Miss Fay, stop him!

(Rudolf *struggles with* Fairy Fay. Miss Mabb *strikes him from behind with a broom. He collapses, dazed, into her arms. She and* Fairy Fay *put him on to a chair*)

* Or other popular astrologer.

Scene 6   THE STORY OF CINDERELLA

FAIRY FAY. Good for you, Miss Mabb.
MISS MABB Quick, tie him up with this invisible rope.

(*They go through the motions of tying him to the chair with a rope.* RUDOLF *sits up*)

(*Hitting him again*) Oh, no, you don't! Tighter, Miss Fay, tighter!

(*They tighten the invisible rope*)

RUDOLF. I'm sure there's a dreadful lump on my head!
MISS MABB. Two lumps.
FAIRY FAY (*picking up Rudolf's paper*) Miss Mabb, look at this! Cinderella's signature—it's disappeared!
MISS MABB (*looking*) Why, so it has! That's strange!
RUDOLF. The stars are indeed against me! Fool that I am, I must have lent her the pen with the patent vanishing ink!
MISS MABB. Vanishing ink! What does this mean?
FAIRY FAY (*looking at the paper over her shoulder*) Look—the words "Magic Shop"—they're all smudged!
MISS MABB. So they are! Why, the ink's still wet! Ah, now I understand! You tricked Cinderella and you thought you'd trick me!
RUDOLF. Mercy! Mercy for a poor misguided fellow-immortal!
MISS MABB. What mercy did you show to me?
RUDOLF. But think of all the dreadful publicity! They'll publish our pictures together!
MISS MABB. Yes! "Local Girl Captures Desperate Criminal!" A splendid advertisement for the Magic Shop!
FAIRY FAY (*at the door*) Some people are coming—in a hurry!
RUDOLF. Oh, dear—the police! Won't you hide me till they've gone?
MISS MABB. How could I do that?
RUDOLF. Lend me your invisible cloak.
MISS MABB. It's at the invisible menders.

(*There is a knock at the door*)

See who that is, Miss Fay—I'll keep an eye on him!
RUDOLF. Oh, dear, they've come to arrest me!
MISS MABB. Very likely.

(FAIRY FAY *ushers in* DANDINI)

DANDINI. Ah, so there you are, you old scoundrel! Congratulations, madam, on a smart capture.
RUDOLF. Foiled—and by a woman!
DANDINI. Squire Rudolf, alias ex-King Rudolf of Pandemonium, alias Count Rudolfo, alias Reckless Rudy, I hereby charge you with high treason, low conduct, riding a whirlwind to the public danger, and travelling on a Corporation trolley-bus*

---

* Or other local bus service.

with intention to avoid payment of fare. What have you to say to the last and gravest charge?

RUDOLF. Not guilty! The conductress she said, "I'm coming up, ducks"—but she never did!

DANDINI. Tell that to the inspector!

(TILDA *bursts in*)

TILDA. Wudy!

RUDOLF. What, is there no end to me torment? Will me black soul never rest in peace?

TILDA. Now, duckie, you just welax and let Tillie take over.

RUDOLF. I plead guilty to everything. Take me away and lock me up—safe!

TILDA. Oo, dear, kind, Mr Dandini, do please give Wudy another chance!

DANDINI. Impossible.

RUDOLF. Out of the question!

DANDINI. He's a scoundrel who deserves no mercy.

RUDOLF. Not a bit!

DANDINI. I'll see that he gets a life sentence.

RUDOLF. Oh, do!

DANDINI (*to Fairy Fay*) Release him, please.

(FAIRY FAY *unties him*)

TILDA. Hooway! (*She grabs Rudolf*)

RUDOLF. Here, what's the idea?

DANDINI (*to Tilda*) Take him away—he's yours!

(HARDUP *enters* R)

RUDOLF. But this is monstrous! I hereby give notice of appeal—if necessary I shall take it to the House of Lords . . .

HARDUP. Here, what's this about my trades union?

DANDINI. Hello, Baron—just in time to congratulate your new son-in-law!

HARDUP. Eh, you don't say! Ah well, what can't be cured must be endured!

RUDOLF. Excuse me, I think I'll just pop out for a quick one. (*He skips to the door*)

TILDA (*grabbing him*) Not without me you don't, ducky! Come on, Mr Dandini—it's Wudy's tweat!

(TILDA *and* DANDINI *go out frog-marching* RUDOLF *between them*)

HARDUP (*to Miss Mabb*) That's better! Now we can have a bit of a talk, like—just you and me, Miss Mabb, eh?

MISS MABB. Miss Fay, isn't there anything you could be doing in the stock-room?

FAIRY FAY. O K. I can take a hint.

(FAIRY FAY *goes out*)

MISS MABB (*coyly*) You were saying, Baron?

HARDUP. How do you do it, Miss Mabb? That's what I want to know—how d'you do it, eh?

MISS MABB (*skittishly*) Oh, diet and exercise, you know—diet and exercise.

HARDUP. What's that got to with Two-Way Communication?

MISS MABB. Oh, you mean on Fairyvision? Well, you know, Baron, we inventors often find ourselves working on parallel lines.

HARDUP. Eh, I wouldn't say that. Parallel lines never meet, you know—not like us, eh?

MISS MABB. I quite agree we might achieve better results if we worked together—pooled our resources, as it were.

HARDUP. You mean—form a limited company?

MISS MABB. What I had in mind was more in the nature of a partnership.

HARDUP. An' not a bad idea at that. After all, man can't live by macklin' alone . . .

MISS MABB. Or woman by magic.

HARDUP. And it'll be lonesome up at Hardup Hall without young Cinders. Tell you what—why don't you and me get wed on same day as her and Prince? Make it a proper do, like?

MISS MABB. An excellent idea. So that's settled, then?

HARDUP (*cautiously*) Aye—so long as you let me in on that Two-Way Communication!

MISS MABB. With pleasure, Baron. As a matter of fact the principle's really very simple.

HARDUP. You don't say?

MISS MABB. Oh yes! You see—Two-Way Communication works like this! (*She pulls* HARDUP *towards her and firmly plants a "smacker" on his cheek*)

CURTAIN

SCENE 7

SCENE—*The Ballroom of the Palace.*
The Ballroom is now gaily decorated.

When the CURTAIN *rises, there is a fanfare.* DANDINI *appears before the* TABS *with a drum. He has drumsticks in his belt and a scroll in his hand. He unrolls the scroll and reads.*

DANDINI. "To whom these Christmas presents come, greeting! Be it known, published and delivered that We, Charming, undoubted Prince of this Land of Fairytale, do request, require and command Our loyal subjects to present themselves without delay at Our Palace Beautiful, there to consume, imbibe and freely partake of the splendid banquet cooked, confected and concocted to celebrate the solemn nuptials of Our Royal Self and The Lady Cinderella, youngest daughter of Our trusty and well-beloved cousin The Baron Hardup of Hardup Hall in this Our realm of Fairytale." (*He rolls up the scroll, tucks it in his belt, wipes his brow and relaxes*) Phew! That's for the record, of course. What it really boils down to is—if you want a bun at the wedding breakfast you'd better look sharp, because the happy couple are just coming out of church. The bride looks positively radiant—no-one would dream it was that ragged little girl. Funny, isn't it, how things have turned out? Why, it would make a regular serial story—or a play. A play! Yes, that's quite an idea! (*He takes the drumsticks from his belt and beats out the rhythm of the Duet*)

No. 11 DUET (DANDINI *and* RUDOLF)

DANDINI.   A Cinderella play,
              A bring-the-children play,
         A neo-Gilbertian and topical version,
               A family-party play!

               A delicate fairy play,
               A will-o'-the-wispy play,
         A Puck-and-Peasblossom, a gauzey-and-gossamer
               Cobwebby kind of play!

The TABS *open on the Ballroom.* FAIRIES, *led by* FAIRY FAY, *enter singing "A delicate fairy play", etc. During the duet each verse is first sung solo, then repeated as chorus while the character indicated enters with appropriate business.*

DANDINI.   A melodramatic play,
              A Twopenny Coloured play,
              A thwarted-desire-of-villainous-Squire,
              A Virtue Triumphant play!

(RUDOLF *enters to Chorus*)

RUDOLF.   A funny and frisky play,
              A jolly and jaunty play,
         A tumble-and-tussle and slap-on-the-bustle,
              A comical kind of play!

(HILDA *and* TILDA *enter to Chorus.* HILDA *joins* DANDINI *and* TILDA, RUDOLF)

DANDINI.   A lend-me-a-hankie play,
              A pluck-at-the-heartstrings play,
         A lover unlucky but lively and plucky—
              A Pag-a-liacci play!

SCENE 7   THE STORY OF CINDERELLA

(BUTTONS, *carrying Cinderella's rose, enters to Chorus*)
RUDOLF.   A highly inventive play,
           A soundly constructed play,
           A fruitful alliance of magic and science—
           A practical sort of play!
(BARON HARDUP *enters to Chorus*)
DANDINI.   A scholarly type of play,
           A cultural class of play,
           A most educational, French-adaptational
           Arts Council choice of play!
(MISS MABB *enters to Chorus and joins Hardup*)
RUDOLF.   A sentimental play,
           A sweet romantic play,
           A lovers-a-clinging and wedding-bells-ringing,
           A happily ending play!
(CINDERELLA *and* PRINCE *enter to Chorus*)
PRINCE.   Welcome, our subjects, to this merry meeting;
           Accept our thanks for your melodious greeting:
           Today a lovely consort we have won,
           And Baron Hardup's gained a royal son.
           Stand forth, our dear papa-in-fairy-lore!
           Who Hardup was, hard up shall be no more,
           But pass creative well-rewarded days
           As Minister of Wonderworks and Ways.
HARDUP.   That's champion—the job I'll soon be tacklin'—
           Eh, yon Department wants a *lot* o' macklin'!
PRINCE (*to Hardup*)
           Our favours shall increase—in proof of which
           We now create you Viscount Veryrich,
           And wish you joy on this your wedding-day
           With our beloved Mabel Mabb.
MISS MABB.   M.A.!
PRINCE.   And now, what says our bride and gentle queen,
           First lady of this Fairytale demesne?
CINDERELLA (*to the Audience*)
           Excuse me if I seem a little shy—
           To public speaking unaccustomed I;
           But still, to point a moral I'll endeavour.
           It is: Although you're neither rich nor clever,
           If you are good, and wash behind your ears,
           And do your sums, without a doubt, my dears,
           Someday, somewhere, you'll certainly discover
           A handsome, rich and well-connected lover.
           Of course it helps, I hardly need remind you,
           If you've a Fairy Godmother behind you!

No. 12 FINALE (THE COMPANY)
(*Reprise of No. 3*)

CINDERELLA. And now on Cind'rella, your little Cind'rella,
It's time for the curtain to fall,
With wedding-bells ringing, and everyone singing,
Good-bye and good luck to you all!
BUTTONS. Yes, good-bye to Buttons—remember poor Buttons
Alas, my romance was ill-starred!
DANDINI. Good-bye to Dandini, obliging Dandini—
Allow me to leave you my card!
RUDOLF. Good-bye to the Squire, that scoundrel and liar!
Believe me, 'twas only my fun!
(*To the Prince*)
A sportsman-like loser, I'll own it to you, sir,
I'm glad that the best lady won!

(*He bows to* MISS MABB, *who curtsies in response*)

CINDERELLA. Good-bye to Cind'rella, your loving Cind'rella—
We're so glad you came to the ball!
Our playtime is ending—the curtain's descending—
A happy New Year to you all!
ALL. Good-bye to Cind'rella, our loving Cind'rella, etc.

CURTAIN

FURNITURE AND PROPERTY PLOTS

ACT I

Scene 1

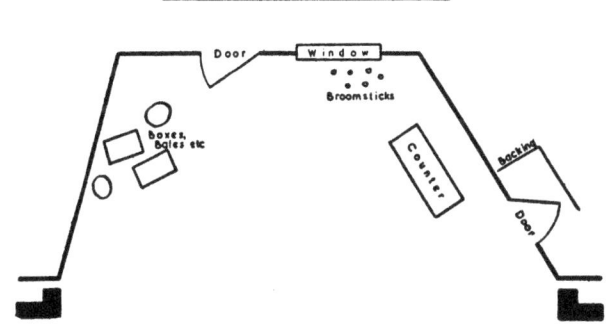

On stage: Brooms, boxes, tins, jars, sacks, etc.
Bale of cloth
Stock-book and pencil on counter
Coat-hangers on rack

Off stage: M.A. robes, wings and fairy wand (Miss Mabb)

Personal: Visiting cards, document, banknotes (Rudolf)
Invitation cards (Dandini)

Scene 3

[Stage plan diagram showing: Garden backing, Window, Fairyvision Set, Kitchen Units, Backing, Door, Fireplace, Stools]

On stage: Fairyvision set
Kitchen units. *To contain:* dough in dish, flour, etc., in patent mixer, frying-pan, cartons, etc., in cupboard, top-hat, cans with liquids and powders overhead, rod with washing
Washing-machine
Several stools
Saw, mallet, etc.
Instruction book
Jar with money on shelf

Off stage: Crockery (BUTTONS)
Basket with groceries (CINDERELLA)
Newspaper (PRINCE)

Personal: Snuff-box (PRINCE)
Coronet, handkerchief (HARDUP)
3 invitation cards (DANDINI)
Coins (BUTTONS)

Scene 4

On stage: Soapbox
Banner

Off stage: Cauldron, fire (FAIRY FAY)
Bicycle, bell (MISS MABB)
Ingredients for potion (FAIRIES)

Scene 5

On stage: Towel
Corsets, tape-measure

THE STORY OF CINDERELLA

        Spanner
        Lamp
        2 bonnets, veils, scarves, 2 pairs of goggles

Set: jam-jar and lamp on shelf

Off stage: Cap, muffler, goggles (HARDUP)
        Mirror, glass slippers (MISS MABB)
        Goblet (FAIRY FAY)
        Cinderella's ball dress, etc. (FAIRIES)
        Tray with pumpkin, rat, mice, lizards (BUTTONS'
        Coach-and-six model

Personal: Rose (CINDERELLA)

ACT II

SCENE 1

On stage: Signpost
        Atommycar
        Telescope in car
        Milestone
        Tools

Personal: Dried peas (HARDUP)

SCENE 2

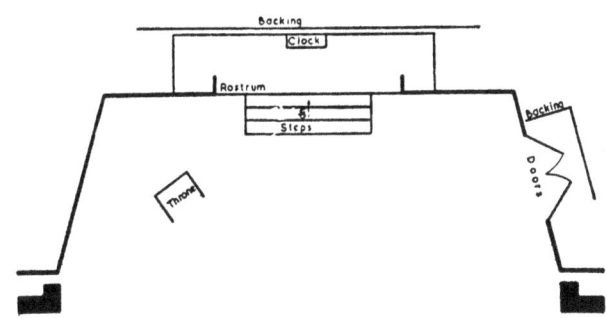

On stage: Clock
        Throne

Off stage: Wine-glasses (BALL GUESTS)
        Tray with wine-glasses (RUDOLF)
        Tray with covers (ATTENDANT)

74 THE STORY OF CINDERELLA

               Opera cloak, moustache (RUDOLF)
               Ragged dress (CINDERELLA)

Personal: Major-domo's wand (DANDINI)
               Novel (PRINCE)
               Trousers (HARDUP)
               Banknote (RUDOLF)
               Roll of banknotes (DANDINI)
               Watch (PRINCE)

SCENE 3

Off stage: Broom with cushion, etc. (BUTTONS)
               Glass slipper (PRINCE)
               2 sacks (MISS MABB, FAIRY FAY)

SCENE 4

On stage: 3 foot-baths
               Mustard tin
               Kettle
               Tablespoon
               Knife
               Medicine bottle, 3 glasses
               2 trays with cups, tumblers, etc.
               Glass slipper on stool

Off stage: Glass slipper (DANDINI)
               Pie to hold slipper

Personal: 2 copies of document (RUDOLF)
               Fountain-pen (RUDOLF)
               Chocolate (BUTTONS)

SCENE 5

Personal: Paper (DANDINI)

SCENE 6

On stage: Fairy wand
               Brooms
               Chair

Off stage: Newspaper (FAIRY FAY)

Personal: Document (RUDOLF)

SCENE 7

Personal: Drum, drumsticks, scroll (DANDINI)
               Rose (BUTTONS)

LIGHTING PLOT

ACT I, SCENE 1

    Fittings required: None
    Interior. Daytime
    The MAIN ACTING AREAS are R, C and LC and L by the counter
    The APPARENT SOURCE OF LIGHT is the window up LC

To open: daylight

No cues

ACT I, SCENE 2

    Fittings required: None
    Exterior. Daytime
    The MAIN ACTING AREA is the front of the stage

To open: daylight

No cues

ACT I, SCENE 3

    Fittings required: None
    Interior. Daytime
    The MAIN ACTING AREAS are down R, up C by the Fairy set, C and up LC by the kitchen units
    The APPARENT SOURCE OF LIGHT is the window UD RC

To open: daylight

No cues

ACT I, SCENE 4

    Fittings required: some form of fire for cauldron
    As Scene 2

ACT I, SCENE 5

    Fittings required: lamp
    Interior. Evening
    The MAIN ACTING AREAS are L, C, and up C and LC
    The APPARENT SOURCE OF LIGHT is the window up RC

To open: evening

Cue: The door R opens
        Bring up strips outside door

ACT II, Scene 1

    Fittings required: none
        Exterior. Evening
        The MAIN ACTING AREA is the front of the stage

To open: evening light

No cues

ACT II, Scene 2

    Fittings required: none
        Interior. Evening
        The MAIN ACTING AREAS cover the whole stage
        The APPARENT SOURCE OF LIGHT is a window in the fourth wall

To open: brightly lit

Cue: The PRINCE and CINDERELLA exit to the banqueting hall
                                                              (page 39)
        *Dim lights to Black-Out. Bring up spot on clock-face while hands move.
        Then take out spot and bring up lights again to full*

ACT II, Scene 3

    As Act I, Scene 4, except that it is now moonlight

No cues

ACT II, Scene 4

    As Act I, Scene 5, except that it is now morning

No cues

ACT II, Scene 5

    Fittings required: none
        Exterior. Daytime
        The MAIN ACTING AREA is the front of the stage

To open: daylight

No cues

ACT II, Scene 6

    As Act I, Scene 1

No cues

ACT II, Scene 7

    As Act II, Scene 2

No cues

www.ingramcontent.com/pod-product-compliance
Ingram Content Group UK Ltd.
Pitfield, Milton Keynes, MK11 3LW, UK
UKHW021845210426
5322IPUK00022B/472